The Power of a Changed Mind

The Power of a Changed Mind
Copyright © 2014
Author: Tiffany Buckner-Kameni
Email: info@anointedfire.com

Cover design: Anointed Fire™ Christian Publishing
Publisher: Anointed Fire™ Christian Publishing
Publisher's Website: www.afirepublishing.com

All scriptures noted in this book were taken from the King James bible unless otherwise noted.

ALL RIGHTS RESERVED. This book contains material protected under International and Federal Copyright Laws and Treaties. Any unauthorized reprint or use of this material is prohibited. No part of this book may be reproduced or transmitted in any form or by any means, electronic or mechanical, including photocopying, recording, or by any information storage and retrieval system without express written permission from the author / publisher.

You may NOT sell or redistribute this book!

ISBN-13: 978-0692307557
ISBN-10: 0692307559

Disclaimer: This book is designed to provide information and motivation to our readers. It is sold with the understanding that the publisher is not engaged to render any type of psychological, legal, or any other kind of professional advice. No warranties or guarantees are expressed or implied by the author, since every man has his own measure of faith. The individual author(s) shall not be liable for any physical, psychological, emotional, financial, or commercial damages, including; but not limited to, special, incidental, consequential or other damages. Our views and rights are the same: You are responsible for your own choices, actions, and results.

Dedication

I dedicate this book to the one and only true and Living GOD, JEHOVAH. Thank you for who You are and everything You've done. You are great and worthy to be praised.

Table of Contents

Introduction..IX
   The Power..1
   The Power of a Changed Mind................................7
   The Power of Beliefs...33
   The Power of Faith..47
   Fear: The Boa Constrictor of Faith........................63
   Deceptive Perception...71
   Defining Moments..79
   Mental Inversion...93
   The Evolution of Mad Science.............................103
   The Power of Imaginations..................................119
   The Horror of Horoscopes...................................133
   Mental Occupation...147
   Life's Mirages...163
   Channeling Spirits..173
   Gender Channeling & Homosexuality................185
   A Changed Reality...203
   As a Man Thinks..211
   Kingdom Thinking...219
   Overcoming Procrastination................................229
   The Power of a Made Up Mind............................249
   The Depth of Understanding...............................259
   The Power of Repetition......................................275
   31 Days to a Renewed Mind................................295

Introduction

Behind every great finish, there was a rocky start and an even rockier journey. You can't simply hope yourself into a better place; you have to actually take each journey one step at a time until you reach your finish line. And the funny part about life is, every finish line we cross marks a new starting point in our journeys. We want to finish and we want to finish at the front of every race we run, but as we grow older, we come to understand that in some races, we'll have to take whatever place GOD gives us, and we need to be thankful to be alive to run another day.

The human mind is amazing. As a matter of fact, the human mind is so complex that scientists have preserved and partially dissected the brain of Albert Einstein because they wanted to compare his brain with the brain of average people. In doing so, scientists hoped to discover some formation or deformation to attribute Einstein's intelligence to. If they could find some form of tissue or some abnormality, they would likely attempt to replicate that tissue or abnormality. At the same time, it would silence the convictions of so many scientists who have not been able to measure up to Einstein's intelligence quotient (I.Q.).

Just what is it about the human mind that separates what the world refers to as geniuses from normal people? And what can a changed mind do for us? The truth is: We all have the ability to be labeled by the world as geniuses, because we all have the ability to learn as much as we want. But the brain is like the body: It usually takes the same journey that our parents' brains took. The people who break away from generational thinking are usually those individuals who's been violently opposed by life; thus, shifted into a different reality than the reality that their parents had. This shift undoubtedly caused them to have to face challenges their parents never faced, meet new personality types, and conform to a whole new environment.

In *The Power of a Changed Mind*, you will learn just how powerful your mind is and how you can activate a change in it. This life-altering read will help you understand why you've been challenged, overcome, and overwhelmed by many of the obstacles that you've had to face in your life.

The Power

What exactly is power? Merriam-Webster defines power as:
- the ability or right to control people or things
- ability to act or produce an effect
- legal or official authority, capacity, or right
- possession of control, authority, or influence over others

So, what exactly is power? Power is the ability to move, create, or change things and people. It is a force exerted from an action that signals a reaction.

We all know that GOD is all-powerful; meaning, HE possess all power. HE created the earth and everything in it simply by speaking it into existence. GOD gave us this very same power. We have the ability to create things through words, beliefs, and through physical force. We have the ability to create people through sex. We have the ability to change our realities by changing our minds. In other words, GOD created mankind much like HIMSELF, and that's why

The Power

HE called us gods.

- → **Psalm 82:6:** I have said, Ye are gods; and all of you are children of the most High.
- → **John 10:34:** Jesus answered them, Is it not written in your law, I said, Ye are gods?

GOD refers to us as "gods" because HE has given us the power to create, and HE has given us dominion over the earth and everything in it.

- → **Genesis 1:26:** And God said, Let us make man in our image, after our likeness: and let them have dominion over the fish of the sea, and over the fowl of the air, and over the cattle, and over all the earth, and over every creeping thing that creepeth upon the earth.
- → **Luke 10:19:** Behold, I give unto you power to tread on serpents and scorpions, and over all the power of the enemy: and nothing shall by any means hurt you.

Because we have power over the earth and everything in it, we have power over the enemy; meaning, Satan is in subjection to the WORD of

The Power

GOD, and if the WORD is in us, Satan has to submit to us. This is one of the reasons that the enemy hates us so much. Think of it this way. What if you were sixteen years old and your parents told your three year old sister that she could tell you what to do? How would you feel having a little sister who doesn't know as much as you and hasn't lived as long as you, all of a sudden telling you what to do? To Satan, you are like that little sister. Of course, Satan knows the Bible inside-out, and he was once a son of GOD, but he betrayed GOD and was cast out of Heaven. Now, there are billions of souls walking about the earth who hasn't been around as long as he has, and most people (if not all) don't know as much as the enemy knows. After all, he lived in Heaven and was in the presence of GOD, so it goes without saying that he doesn't like the fact that we have been given authority over him. Nevertheless, the LORD has given us power over the enemy and power over everything in the earth. But when we use this power for evil, we become guilty of witchcraft, thus causing us to work against GOD and not for HIM.

Just as we have the ability to change things, we have the ability to change our minds, but most people fear

The Power

change because any changes made to the mind equate to changes to ones' reality. We are creatures (created ones) who adapt easily to good and bad situations, and anytime we adapt to a situation, we oftentimes make our homes in those situations and mindsets. That's because we've learned to exist in our realities, no matter how bleak they appear.

Our lives are nothing more than a series of beliefs and decisions that have come together to form our realities. Of course, our decisions are centered on our beliefs, and sometimes, our beliefs are established after we've seen the consequences of our decisions. Every good and bad thing that has ever happened to us has had some impact on our thinking patterns and beliefs. To this day, our realities are nothing more than the consequences of our beliefs and choices. You'll notice that the word "sequence" is found in the word "consequence". This indicates that our consequences are nothing more than a sequence of reactions that have taken place because of our actions. In other words, consequences are life's way of responding to our choices, movements, and words.

Every Word that proceeds from the mouth of GOD

The Power

has absolute power, and will return to GOD having accomplished everything it was sent out to accomplish. For this reason, GOD wants us to learn the WORD so that we can utilize this power in our lives, but if we don't believe in GOD or HIS WORD, we can't utilize the power of HIS WORD. That's why the enemy attacks our belief systems so mercilessly. Satan is determined to make sure you doubt GOD and never realize the power that is already within you. He works tirelessly to find ways to discredit the scriptures so that you and all of mankind will not recognize the fact that believers have authority over him. Satan tried to use his power of will against GOD, and of course, he failed. He was cast into the earth, and for a short time, he ruled the earth. Suddenly, CHRIST came and took the power from Satan and gave it to those who believed in HIM; meaning, Satan not only lost his glorious title in Heaven, but he also lost his self-erected title in the earth. But a man who doesn't know he's a king will foolishly submit to a servant; therefore, Satan does not want us (believers) to know that we are kings and queens. If you don't know who you are, Satan will happily assign you to work for his kingdom, but make no mistake about it, he still hates you because of who you are.

The Power

You have the ability to change your life and everything in it by simply changing your mind. Sure, pursuing a changed mind isn't exactly an easy feat, considering we are creatures of habit, and we oftentimes default to what we know. Nevertheless, we can still change by creating new habits and being willing to persistently and consistently pursue change.

The Power of a Changed Mind

I sat in the car next to a man I'd just met. He was very handsome, and I couldn't identify with him. I was about eighteen years old or younger, and I'd been accustomed to dating thug types. But the guy I was seated next to was different. He was dressed to impress, well groomed, obviously wealthy, and very well spoken. I felt a little intimidated by him because I didn't know what to say to such a character, so I put on my shy face. It worked. He thought I was shy, so he began saying all of the wrong things to me. Truthfully, if any other guy had said the things he was saying, I would have let off a fury of choice words at him, exited the car, and never spoke with him again, at least not intentionally. But I sat next to a man I could not relate to, so curiosity got the best of me. I smiled, dropped my head, and giggled with every foolish word he let out of his mouth. "Oh. You're the shy type," he said with a smile. I grinned and meekly nodded my head in affirmation. Truthfully, I was nowhere near shy; I just didn't know how to identify with him, so I pretended to be shy. That was my way

The Power of a Changed Mind

of going undercover to find out whom he was underneath.

He turned my right arm to read my tattoo. "Oh, so you're scandalous?" he asked. I felt uncomfortable at that moment. Was my cover blown? Would he suddenly realize that I wasn't shy and start digging for the real me? I'd purposely hid who I was under many layers of hurt, games, and whatever I could find to keep the real me from coming to the surface. "I just liked that word. I got it off a Prince C.D.," I responded.

One game I played that I found was very effective was playing the shy and somewhat innocent girl. What I found back then was that people would be their wicked selves around shy people because they feel no need to hide with a person who's scared to be themselves. My new friend was obviously a talker and he loved to meet women he could feel superior around. After listening to him pompously go on and on about himself and his accomplishments, I decided to swoop in and say what I was thinking. After all, I could tell that he wasn't the relationship type, but he was handsome, rich, and a complete mystery to me. I told him that I knew that he wasn't looking for a relationship and neither was I, but I'd come to realize

The Power of a Changed Mind

that I was going from one relationship to the next and I didn't want to have sex with every man that I dated. I wanted to find one man that I could be with while I dated around; that way, I wouldn't get the "whore" tag. Of course, he agreed.

From that moment on, I stopped liking thug types because I'd met and begun to entertain a different type of man. I realized that I could attract a whole different breed of men; men who would be leaders and great providers for their families someday. I would occasionally date someone who was thuggish, but I found that I had no respect for such characters because I'd sampled another world. And just like that, I was no longer interested in getting tattoos or even listening to rap music. I began to listen to music that I knew would appeal to the type of man I wanted for myself. I didn't care if he was rich or not. I just wanted him to be a leader who knew what he wanted.

I was demonically infested back then. My thinking was completely perverted, and I was a woman of wiles and games because I lacked wisdom. Most people who knew me had written me off as a lost cause. Don't get me wrong: I was a decent girl underneath it

The Power of a Changed Mind

all. I wanted to be married, have children, and give my life to the LORD, but I'd lived a rough life. I'd been hurt so much that I'd begun to bury the real me underneath many faces and personalities. I didn't know it then, but I was looking for love. At the same time, there were many strongholds in my mind, and one of those strongholds was an addiction to sex. The ironic twist in it all, however, was that I didn't want the "whore" tag associated with me. I'd witnessed firsthand that trying to silence the "sex monster" wasn't working.

In sin, I continued to climb the ladder towards death. That ladder looks like an elevator, but in truth, it's the stairway to hell. Every time I learned something new, I tried something new. My "type" continued to change and my way of speaking began to change. I no longer had to speak thug lingo; I only needed to speak proper English and dress like a professional woman to get the "type" of man I wanted. My whole life was centered around being in a relationship and having fun.

When I began to go to church, I was serious about giving my life to the LORD, but it wasn't easy. I went

The Power of a Changed Mind

to church and looked at the many men sitting in the sanctuary, and I thought to myself *I want one of those types of men.* I thought like that because I wasn't whole yet. Nevertheless, I decided to stay focused. I wanted to see if there was any help for me; after all, I thought I was beyond repair. I'd tried everything that I could think of. I'd tried going cold turkey without sex; I tried offering myself to one man while dating others, I'd even tried dating men who I wasn't the least bit attracted to, but nothing helped. That was, until I tried JESUS.

Don't get me wrong. Going to church wasn't nearly enough. Who I was becoming was battling with who I'd become. My flesh didn't let go easily; Satan didn't let go easily, but I was determined to overcome the demons that were haunting me.

I began going to church often, and with each visit, GOD began to put me back together again. I didn't stop fornicating immediately. As a matter of fact, I married twice while I was still in the deliverance phases. But GOD continued to work on me. HE never left nor forsook me. As I began to read my Bible even more, I found myself wanting to please GOD more

The Power of a Changed Mind

than I wanted to please myself. Those overbearing sexual desires completely got up and fled and every time GOD delivered me from a mindset, HE explained what HE'D delivered me from. I came to understand that I wasn't addicted to sex. I wanted to be loved, and sex afforded me opportunities to feel loved, if but for a few minutes. My soul hungered for love, and many of the behaviors in sex mimicked the behaviors associated with Eros (romantic love).

By the time I met and married my second husband, I was a completely different woman than I was when I'd met and married my first husband; nevertheless, I still wasn't whole yet. During that second marriage, I began to grow up rapidly in the WORD because by that time, I'd started having an actual relationship with GOD that stretched outside the four walls of the sanctuary. Within a year of marrying my second husband, I was no longer the woman that he'd married. I'd been transformed by the renewing of my mind. I knew within my mind and heart that I wouldn't fornicate if I was single again. I began to go through a time of sorrow; a time in which I repented and begged GOD repeatedly for HIS forgiveness. Finally, I was at a time in my life that I understood why GOD said not to fornicate. I loved GOD more and I wanted to please HIM with my life. Of course, GOD had already forgiven me, but it took a long time for me to forgive myself.

By the second year of my marriage, I was sure I'd made a huge mistake. I had been through a spiritual awakening, and I didn't like what I was waking up to. The more I testified about what GOD had delivered me from, the more GOD healed and delivered me. The more GOD delivered me, the less I found I had in common with the people in my life, one of those people being the man I'd chosen for myself. Nevertheless, I had to submit wholly to GOD and ask for HIS direction. I didn't want to make anymore mistakes. I only wanted to glorify HIS Name in my words and actions. And just like that, my mind changed... again.

The point is: There was a time when I was not old enough to make a mature decision for my life because I didn't know who I was going to grow up (in the LORD) to be. I kept finding friends and entering relationships, according to the level I was in when I was lost, but once I found the LORD and HE

The Power of a Changed Mind

delivered me, I stopped looking for people on my level. I started asking GOD to place, replace, and remove the people going in and out of my life according to HIS plan for my life, and not my own plans. You see, when we are lost, we find people who we believe will serve as great life partners for our own plans, but once GOD starts delivering us, HE has to deliver us from those people who we'd chosen for ourselves. They represent who we'd learned to be, not who we truly are. I've had many not-so-good friends that I've had to let go of, but I didn't do this until I was on the path of faith. Each new door represented a new opportunity for me, and I began to discover that I couldn't go through certain doors unless I let go of certain people and certain mindsets. At the same time, I came to each new door that was presented to me with the knowledge of what I'd been through, but the understanding didn't come until I obediently walked through those doors. I survived, not just to live another day, but also to understand the days I'd lived.

I changed my mind. It was as simple as that. Of course, GOD renewed my mind; therefore, HE gets the glory, but HE gave me the choice to either stay in

The Power of a Changed Mind

the old ways of thinking or enter a new and unfamiliar way of thinking. It wasn't easy because anyone who's accustomed to living and thinking a certain way is comfortable in their lifestyles and mindsets. Anytime we're shifted to the unfamiliar, we leave our comfort zones and have no choice but to step out on faith.

When my second husband lived in Germany, I would often go to visit him for months at a time, and even though I loved Germany, I refused to live there. I didn't want to live in Germany because I didn't understand the language, the people, nor did I understand their culture. This is to say that we can be presented with comfortable situations, but we often shy away from them because they are foreign to us. The average person wants to be in control of everything, and the average person has set their lives up in a way that they can be and feel in control of their lives. But GOD calls us to come outside of average, and this means, we have to give up the control we've learned to love in order to be shifted into new territories, new lifestyles, and new mindsets. When I worked at Wal-Mart, I was nothing more than a lost soul, but I was bold enough to want something different for my life, even though I'd never been to college. I had enough faith in me to

The Power of a Changed Mind

understand that I didn't have to let society or my lack of a college degree dictate my future. I broke the mold, and in doing so, I offended many people who'd carved out a place for me in the molds they lived in.

What happens as you change your mind?
- You will go through moments of uncertainty, but that's great. GOD told you to walk by faith and not by sight.
- You'll offend your family. There are many people in your family who'd pretty much written you off. They've identified you according to the personalities they've seen on you, but they cannot identify who you really are. Here's the thing: GOD often hides who we are from those closest to us because sometimes, those people are closest to the devil himself.
- You'll offend and lose many friends. I knew in my heart that I was going to be successful. I'd known that pretty much all of my life because GOD told me that. I used to say that I was going to bless the people in my life because they were there with me when I had nothing. Little did I know that they'd walk away or have to be removed when GOD began to make

something out of me. People will often love who you are, or at least tolerate who you are, but they can't understand who you are becoming.

- You're going to be so surprised that you may question your own sanity. As my mind changed, I kept enduring moments of awkwardness because I didn't recognize the girl I was becoming. There were many times that I questioned myself, my salvation, my deliverance, and my choices because I kept seeing so many changes and they were all new to me. But I did know to go to the Throne of GOD and ask HIM what was happening, and HE summed it up in two beautiful words: You're changing.
- Others will question your sanity or deliverance, or at least, pretend to do so. When you begin to leave people behind, it goes without saying that they'll be offended. Especially if they see you being elevated. People don't actually mind you disassociating from them if you're not doing well or if you're being demoted. It's when you're being promoted that you are the most offensive. That's because people often feel

The Power of a Changed Mind

entitled to whatever GOD is giving you. They tell themselves that they've stuck it out with you for many years, given you whatever they've given you, done for you whatever they've done for you, and tolerated you when you were almost intolerable. For that reason, they begin to think like the scorned wife of a rich man. They think they are entitled to half of what you have, even if that's just fifty bucks and a sandwich. People will say or do anything they believe will have enough rise in it to grow up and be an obstacle to you. Those who were closest to you know just where your soft spots are or where they were, so they'll often throw darts (words, accusations, punches) at what they believe to be your weak spots.

- You'll get a GOD'S-eye view of life, and this isn't always pretty. As I began to change, I found myself thinking that church and church people would be loving and welcoming, but I was wrong. When I was lost, dirty, and seemingly beneath some people, I was welcomed with hugs and supportive words. I was embraced and accepted because I was nothing more than a reason for them to feel good about themselves. I was a charity case, and many believers think that by giving someone a hug and a few encouraging words that they've earned their pass to Heaven. But the moment GOD began to promote me, I got a different view of those same people, and it was not in the least bit pretty. Many were offended because they'd seen me as nothing more than a partying, promiscuous girl who didn't have a hope in this world, but GOD saw something else. Just like HE sees what's on the inside of you because HE put it there.

- Your language will begin to change. Of course, you'll speak English (if that's what you speak), but you'll also learn to speak in faith and faith is a different language than English, French, Spanish, German, or the like. Truthfully, there were many times that I felt bad for not having used my time in Germany to learn to speak German. Had I learned to speak the language, I would have been able to reach out to so many people that I couldn't ordinarily reach out to. That's what faith does. You'll be able to reach people that you weren't ordinarily able to reach when you were in your old mindset. New

The Power of a Changed Mind

mindsets represent new opportunities.
- You'll become more of a threat to the enemy. For every (Godly) change of mind you endure, you become more of a soldier in the army of the LORD. For this reason, you'll notice that the enemy's attacks are fiercer than before, but they won't have as much impact on you. Satan's darts won't pierce you anymore, because you'll be wearing the whole armor of GOD. That's when you'll notice that many of the attacks that would have ordinarily crippled your life in your old way of thinking don't really impact you in your new way of thinking. You'll brush it off and keep on living.
- People will persecute you. Let's face it: They persecuted and hated the WORD HIMSELF: JESUS CHRIST. When you come forth with the WORD in you, they will hate you, but not because of you, because of HIS Name's sake; meaning, they will hate the WORD in you. So, people will speak evil of you, and many of those people will be church-going, bible-toting, scripture-quoting souls who look holy, but make no mistake about it, they will be wolves in sheep's clothing. They'll hate you because you

The Power of a Changed Mind

can see who they are; therefore, you can expose who they are. The more of a threat you are to the enemy, the more he'll threaten you. No worries. Satan's empty words can't do anything with a WORD-filled believer.

- People will mislabel you. As human beings, we like to categorize every person we meet. As GOD changes you, fewer people will be able to relate to you, but people don't know what to do with people they can't understand, so they label them according to their misunderstandings. They'll happily tell you their perceptions of you in an attempt to get you to fit into the labels they've created for you. The more you resist, the more you will be despised amongst men. There's a boldness that will rise in you, and you won't care what people say or think because you'll be focused on making an impact not an impression.

- You'll forgive easier because you'll love more. The closer I got to the LORD, the less I argued with people and the more I loved people. I began to understand that people are at varying stages in their walks of faith; therefore, people will address me according to their levels. I was

The Power of a Changed Mind

once lost and I didn't always receive people well, so I'm not offended nowadays when I'm not received well. At the same time, you'll forgive those who have hurt and betrayed you because understanding will replace the questions you have.

- You'll be able to reach and do more. The opportunities are endless. You won't doubt yourself because you won't depend on yourself; you'll depend on GOD. After you've tasted and seen that the LORD is good, there is no turning back. You will want more of HIM, and you will seek to do more for HIM.

A changed mind is amazing, but just like exercise, it requires a lot of work, sweat, and tears. The average person keeps the same mindset for the rest of his or her life because it's a comfortable place to be, but GOD didn't call you to be average; HE called you to be super-average. There are many things in your heart that you want to do, and fear has kept you from doing them, but I challenge you to do them anyway. Get rid of the people who make you feel awkward when you want to go higher in the LORD and higher in life.

The Power of a Changed Mind

As a photographer, I've noticed that many people book photography sessions with people they don't feel comfortable with. They book these sessions, but when they come to the sessions, they aren't their happiest or their most comfortable selves. That's because the people they've come to the photography sessions with have made them feel like nothing more than living jokes. Consider that friend who laughs when you're about to take your picture, and she blurts out, "Why are you smiling like that?" Her goal was to sow a seed in your mind to stop you from having a beautiful photo. Oftentimes, such a small seed has a huge impact on a person's self perception and self esteem, and characters who sow those seeds were themselves sown in our lives by the enemy.

> → **Matthew 13:24-30:** Another parable put he forth unto them, saying, "The kingdom of heaven is likened unto a man, which sowed good seed in his field: But while men slept, his enemy came and sowed tares among the wheat, and went his way. But when the blade was sprung up, and brought forth fruit, then appeared the tares also. So the servants of the householder came and said unto him, 'Sir,

The Power of a Changed Mind

didst not thou sow good seed in thy field? From whence then hath it tares?' He said unto them, 'An enemy hath done this.' The servants said unto him, 'Wilt thou then that we go and gather them up?' But he said, 'Nay, lest while ye gather up the tares, ye root up also the wheat with them. Let both grow together until the harvest: and in the time of harvest I will say to the reapers, Gather ye together first the tares, and bind them in bundles to burn them: but gather the wheat into my barn.'"

How do you change your mind? It seems easy enough, right? But it isn't because whatever we have in us, we keep defaulting back to until our minds have been renewed. So, what you ought to seek is the WORD of GOD, and ask HIM to give you a renewed mind. Whenever you try to stop doing something and fail, don't give up and tell yourself that you can't quit, simply keep trying to quit over and over again until your mind gives in. You can be any and everything you want to be with a changed mind. This isn't just some famous cliché; it's the truth. If I can be a woman who didn't finish High School, didn't go to college; a woman who'd been molested countless times, raped

The Power of a Changed Mind

a few times; a woman who was broken, promiscuous, and conniving; a woman whose favorite past time was sex; a woman who grew up in a dysfunctional home with dysfunctional thinking, and get past all of that to become who I am today, you can also get past your shortcomings. For every shortcoming you have, GOD has an opportunity to glorify HIS Name. You see, every time you get past something, you get the blessed opportunity to help others get past it. As of today, I own multiple businesses, I've written more than twenty books, and I have a flourishing ministry. Why? Because I took every painful thing that ever happened to me, and I laid it at the altar of GOD. I didn't let society dictate who I'd become. Growing up, I'd heard many things that people predicted would happen to me. One family member tried to speak HIV over me because she didn't like me, and this was before I became sexually active (on purpose). Before then, however, I'd been molested and raped. People often ask me why I don't get up and go back to school, and my question is: For what? GOD is getting the glory for EVERYTHING I am today; not man! I'm not against school, but I wouldn't take what GOD has given me and make it seem as if a man gave it to me when he didn't. No man did for me what GOD has

The Power of a Changed Mind

done for me. HE delivered me from the hands of my enemies. HE delivered me from the powers of darkness. HE delivered me from the people who loved my anointing, but hated my soul. HE delivered me from the soul ties that once stood guard over my soul. HE delivered me from promiscuity. HE delivered me from brokenness, unforgiveness, and wrongful thinking. HE delivered me and then, HE changed my mind. Why in the world would I let man even remotely take that glory away from HIM?

How do you allow GOD to affect a change in your life?

1. Stop being ashamed of your testimony. I spent years worrying about what folks thought about me, but I asked GOD to remove that way of thinking from me and HE did. Now, I testify with no shame; therefore, people no longer have power over me.
2. Get up and be who GOD has called you to be, even when it's uncomfortable. I understand that the last time you tried to change, you lost a few friends, upset a few family members, and stirred up hell against you, but let the folks go who need to be let go of. Love them, but know this: It's okay to love folks from a distance.

The Power of a Changed Mind

You'll know just how far of a distance you need between you and them based on the impact they make on your life and your emotions because of their decisions and words. If what they say or do affects you, they're too close.

3. Don't worry about what people think. People will say and do whatever they want to say and do based on the conditions of their hearts. For example, some family members will ridicule you for distancing yourself from them. Should you care what they say or do? No. Roosters always crow when the sun rises, but that doesn't stop the sun from rising each day. Please understand that many people will have something to say, especially those who feel entitled to your space in life, your anointing, or your possessions. The others who'll speak are oftentimes the ones who've written you off and feel upset about the fact that you weren't the failure they'd predicted you'd be. Let them crow, but you continue to rise and shine as GOD has called you to do.

4. Forgive others. Please ask GOD to put forgiveness in your heart towards anyone who's hurt you and ask HIM to activate that

forgiveness in your life. At first, it'll feel strange because your old understanding may try to resurrect itself and say to you that you're stupid for not taking revenge or reacting, but GOD has a plan for them, and it involves your obedience to HIM.

5. Ask GOD to position the people who are in your life according to HIS will, even if that means removing some or all of the people in your life. You'd be amazed just how much of a hindrance one person could be.

6. Open up your mind to new possibilities. Because of the way I'd grown up, and the people I'd grown up around, ordinarily, I was supposed to be limited in my thinking. I used to say I would never board an airplane or get on a cruise ship. Because I allowed my understanding to go far outside of what I was taught and what was expected of me, GOD took me places that I thought I'd never go, and HE blessed me to do things I thought I'd never do. Don't limit yourself to what you know. Look to learn something new every day of your life. Make a calendar or a daily mind menu where you schedule what you'll be feeding your mind

that day, in addition to the WORD of GOD.
7. Never go one day without reading the WORD and praying to GOD.
8. Establish a real relationship with GOD and not a religious one.
9. Don't look at where you've been or where you haven't been, look to the hills from whence cometh your help, your help cometh from the LORD. As I stated, I didn't finish High School, and not because I wasn't smart enough, but because I wasn't driven enough. That didn't limit me, however. Instead, I learned graphic design from the comfort of my own home, and of course, the HOLY SPIRIT taught me to do every good thing I know how to do today.
10. Don't look at where your parents have or have not been. Sometimes, GOD will use you to be the one to introduce a change to your parents. In many cases, people spend their lives so mad at their parents about what they did or did not do for them, and this is unfortunate because they don't know what GOD will use them to do for their parents. Our parents made mistakes, but they did what they knew how to do according to their understandings at the

The Power of a Changed Mind

time. Forgive them and share the WORD with them. If GOD tells you to separate yourself from them, then do so. But don't look at your parents' limitations and claim them as your own.

Your changed mind is awaiting you. Don't consider where you are today. As a matter of fact, if you're saved, sanctified, and filled with the HOLY SPIRIT, please don't ever get to the place where you think your mind doesn't need renewing. I can't tell you how many renewing processes I've been through, even after I was recognizably a different person inside and out. No matter where you go, be willing to go further in the LORD. The average believer parks in one realm of thinking and they refuse to go any further, and that's when they began to become religious in their thinking. You'll offend religious thinkers, as you are elevated in the LORD, but don't let them get to you. They are simply responding in accordance with their limited understandings. Once you step outside of a man's understanding, you'll step into his perception. Inside of a man's perception are two things: (1) His willingness to reconcile with you if you allow yourself to be fitted into and groomed by his perception, and

(2) His willingness to disassociate himself from you if you continue to be someone he doesn't understand. When given the choice, choose to obey GOD and offend the man.

The Power of Beliefs

One belief will set the stage for every choice you make in your life. All the same, one belief shattered by the truth could destroy every reality you've come to accept.

To believe means to accept something as true. The earth is one big store, and every thing, every thought, and every person you will ever meet in your life is an item in that store. Whatever you believe is what you have bought, and you will take those things with you. Additionally, you will pay the price for every thing, person, and thought you have accepted.
Once you accept someone in your life, that person now has direct access to your heart: the very control center of your life. Once you accept some thing in your life, that thing now has influential power and it will be the foundation for many of the decisions that you will come to make in your life. Additionally, every thought that presents itself to you is auditioning for a role in your heart. If that thought is allowed in or believed, that thought will manifest itself as your

The Power of Beliefs

reality and will shape every future decision you will ever make.

We know that the Bible talks about the heart of a man, but when we read the Bible and witness what it says about the heart, it's easy to see that the Bible speaks of the heart as if it were the brain. That's because the heart is the engine of our lives. It is the central point from which everything flows. That's why those red organs in our chests are referred to as our hearts. Our cardiovascular system is where all of our blood flows from, and it supplies blood to every organ in our bodies. For this reason, we cannot live without our physical hearts.

When the Bible speaks of the heart of a man, it is speaking of his belief system. The mind and the heart are connected, but any information that introduces itself to the mind has no impact in our lives until we believe that information into our hearts. When new information begins to dance around in our minds, we have to choose whether we want to reject or accept that information. To reject something means that we are calling it a lie; therefore, guarding our hearts from it. To believe something is to accept that thing as true, and to allow it into our hearts to become a foundation or a part of every decision we will make in your lives. Something as minute as believing that spinach is dangerous for you is powerful enough to impact a change in your life.

> → **Proverbs 4:23:** Keep thy heart with all diligence; for out of it are the issues of life.

It is of no wonder that GOD told us to guard our hearts, for whatever we believe will directly affect our relationship with HIM. At the same time, anytime a lie is believed in, that lie will begin to wage war with every truth that's found in our hearts.

How Our Beliefs Affect Our Relationships
If you've ever been married, you will know just how important trust is in a marriage. To trust a person means to accept what that person says as true, even if what they said is in past, present, or future tense. For example, if you are a wife and your husband told you that he was going to visit his cousin, you will accept what he is saying as true or you will determine that what he is saying is false. Additionally, you may question what he is saying. If you question what he is

The Power of Beliefs

saying, you are simply indicating that you have neither accepted his words as true or untrue. If you believe he's a liar or you think he may be lying to you, the very foundation of your marriage will come up for questioning.

Pay attention to the words "trust" and "true". You'll notice that they are both similar as they both start with the same first three letters: t-r-u. That's because the foundation of trust is the truth, and without truth, there can be no trust. It is very important for spouses to trust one another, just as it is very important for spouses to be truthful with one another. Once the trust is gone in a marriage, the natural behavior of the human mind is to challenge the marriage in the very same way it challenges new thoughts. For example, if a man believes his wife has been untruthful to him, he will begin to slowly reject her as his wife. Again, this is normal, protective behavior, and it's designed to preserve us. If the husband does not believe his wife, everything he once believed about her will begin to fall apart and his perception of her will change as he attempts to adjust to whatever information he's accepting as truth. Please understand that the human mind needs, craves, searches for, and will stalk the truth with no mercy. But when we can't seem to get the truth out of the people we love, we begin to take whatever facts we've accepted as truth and compare them to what we've been told by our spouses. It is then that we reconsider old information that once attempted to enter our minds, and we'll compare that information with what we think we know, and this is how we draw conclusions. Once a conclusion has been drawn, we establish what we believe as truth in our lives.

How Our Beliefs Affect Who We Choose to Marry
Have you ever noticed that some of the people you once had major crushes on are now people you wouldn't give a second look? It's not that their physical appearances have changed; the problem oftentimes is: Your mind has changed. Your attraction to them during your crush phase was merely based on some quality you believed they had that would compensate for whatever quality you felt you lacked. For example, if you were a meek, quiet woman and a hopeless romantic, you'd likely found yourself crushing on the strong, outspoken man who appeared to have had life figured out. It's not that he was the best-looking man you'd ever seen; the issue was he

The Power of Beliefs

had qualities you felt that you were missing in your life. You were fearful and timid; whereas, he was fearless and bold. In this, you were actually looking to be completed. You felt that he'd bridge the parts of your life that stopped you from achieving your goals. That's why we oftentimes had major crushes on celebrities. At some point, they acted in roles as the very characters we felt we needed in our lives, or they sang songs that cast them as the very characters we felt we needed in our lives. This is the act of being charmed, or better yet, bewitched.

At every point in our lives, we are considering our next step. Each day presents the opportunity for us to plan our tomorrows, and we take the information that we've accepted as truths, and we allow those truths to determine our next step. So, if we believe that the person courting us is everything we want and will ever want in a spouse, we may consider marrying that person or having children with them. Once we take what we are considering and compare it with our imaginations, our new partners' plans and our realities, we will then make a decision. Let's say that you are a man who's decided that you want to marry your girlfriend. Chances are, you've looked at how

The Power of Beliefs

well she has fit into your life, and because you believe your life, mind, and reality will remain the same, you have considered marriage. Again, she's a great fit for you today, but marriages are shaken when our minds, lives, and realities are suddenly changed, and the people we've chosen to be our spouses no longer fit into our new realities.

Most people have voids, and because they have voids, they look for void-fillers. These fillers oftentimes come in the form of relationship partners. If you were a woman who's been molested, and you hadn't healed emotionally, you'd likely enter a relationship with someone you feel can protect and understand you. If you were a man who's been mistreated by his mother, you'd likely enter a relationship with someone you feel you can control. You'd take that woman and use her to fill your voids, but as life proves that your new wife is not able to fill those voids, you will likely become enraged with her. At one point, you thought she was the cure for all of your pain and trust issues, but because you've realized your pain and trust issues are only intensified by your fears of losing her, you'll likely take to striking her, monitoring her activities, and trying to grasp every measure of control over her that you can grab on to. She will undoubtedly pay for the mistakes of your mother. When you married her, you believed that she was the cure, the problem-solver, and your new hero. After marrying her, you discovered that she was just another woman, and could not fill the shoes you'd given to her. You want her in the house where you can see her at all times, but she wants to get out of the house sometimes. This divide will bring about a war that oftentimes ends in divorce or the termination of someone's life.

When we believe that we are ready to be married, we are in the same believing that our minds won't change, but our realities will. Our lack of knowledge will oftentimes send us into emotional whirlwinds where we allow our imaginations to run rampart with thoughts of the future we want to have with our love interests. What we see in our imaginations is standing on the foundations of what we believe and what we want to believe.

How Our Beliefs Affect Our Relationship With GOD

Our belief in GOD and every WORD that proceeded

The Power of Beliefs

from HIS mouth is called faith. We either believe HIM or we don't. The truth is: The average believer has trouble believing GOD; nevertheless, when a person says they believe in GOD and they believe that JESUS CHRIST is the Son of GOD, HE died on the cross for our sins, and rose on the third day, we call them believers. Honestly, many people who proclaim to believe in the LORD are not actual believers because they are attempting to separate GOD from HIS WORD. They believe in GOD, but they don't believe HIS WORD is truth. How so? They repeatedly and rebelliously sin against HIM while quoting the sinner's national anthem: *GOD knows my heart.* They go to church and perform rituals of worship without having a heart of worship. When found in the midst of a trial, they follow the lead of their fears; all the while, rejecting faith. After all, one must be full of faith in order to be faithful. In other words, we must have the WORD of GOD in us, and we must believe HIS WORD if we want to overcome every obstacle that threatens us. If we believe the threat that the obstacle imposes, we are in the same saying that we do not believe GOD, and just like our relationship with our spouses, we must have trust in our relationship with GOD in order for that relationship to work. If we don't trust HIM, our perception of HIM will change, and we will treat HIM in accordance with our fears and doubts, rather than our faith. In other words, we begin to treat HIM like a spouse who is unworthy of our trust. We begin to question HIM, doubt HIM, and call HIM the one thing it is impossible for HIM to be: a liar.

How Our Beliefs Affect Our Lives

Every one of us has desires, and each of those desires has foundations. To build these foundations, something or a series of things occurred. Sometimes, the occurrence was a beautiful event that we wanted to relive, and then, there were those times where a traumatic event occurred that we wanted to prevent. We took those events and we began to build on them. What's amazing about the human mind is it can take a series of traumatic events and create a positive desire because of those events. For example, take a child who's been bullied all of his life. He didn't have the money or the fancy clothes that his peers had, and because of this, he was mocked. He was shunned and looked upon as an outcast, so he learned to entertain himself. He then grew up, went to college, and made a decent life for himself, but he never forgave those children who shunned him as a child. Suddenly, he's climbing the ranks at work, getting into politics, and going back to school. He desires to get married to a beautiful woman, have intelligent children, and provide a life for his family that he couldn't have as a child. Because he never forgave his tormentors, he will live a life that looks good from the outside, but anyone inside his life will suffer because of his unforgiveness. He will live vicariously through his sons; providing them with the life he couldn't have, and attempting to right many of the wrongs he'd suffered when he was young. He will teach his daughters to be nothing more than shallow, educated women who base their worth on their achievements in life. He'll likely choose a beautiful wife who does not love him, but loves what he can provide for her. Because of this, he will mistreat his wife, often subjecting her to a series of adulterous affairs. He will also make his wife pay for the rejections he endured by other beautiful women when he had absolutely nothing. She will become his sounding board; a human microphone doomed to receive and mentally record every complaint, fear, and hateful thing he's ever harbored in his heart. What you see is a man who's got dreams and desires,

The Power of Beliefs

but because the foundation of those dreams and desires is hatred, he will become a driven, but hateful man.

Every occurrence in your life has set you up to be who you are at this very moment. What you believe is directly linked to what you have witnessed, endured, or been told. Of course, when the WORD of GOD began to come into your heart, it began to uproot many of the lies you were told. You've endured trials as each of those lies were unearthed. Those trials weren't kicked off by the unearthing of lies; they were kicked off by your refusal to accept the truth. In other words, each lie died slowly, and you felt the impact of every painful blow because you were still harboring (or believing) those lies in your heart. One thing you'll discover is that even in traumatic events, accepting the truth will help you to face every new revelation. Accepting the truth lessens the pain of betrayal; whereas, holding on to lies causes the process of revelation to be slow and drawn out. It is similar to dying a slow and torturous death.

Anything you have believed into your heart is going to be a part of your heart and choices until you reject it.

The Power of Beliefs

Consider the popular witch's fable that states that if a person breaks a mirror, they will suffer bad luck for seven years. Of course, we know this is a lie, but if you believe that lie, you'd find yourself worried if you were to break a mirror. You may not say it aloud, but in your heart, doubt and fear will begin to rise up, and this will shape your reality. From that point on, every bad occurrence that befalls you would be attributed to that broken mirror. In believing the witch's fable, you will give the enemy a free pass to kick your butt for seven years. In that time, he will likely place another mirror on your path so that you can stay bound by your fears for an additional seven years. This means that by receiving the report of Satan, you would have rejected the truth: the WORD of GOD.

The Power of Faith

→ **Luke 6:45:** A good man out of the good treasure of his heart bringeth forth that which is good; and an evil man out of the evil treasure of his heart bringeth forth that which is evil: for of the abundance of the heart his mouth speaketh.

To be faithful means to be full of faith. To be faithful means to be consistently and habitually the same to a default. For example, if you'd ever been worldly and full of profane words, by default, you probably cursed when you stumped your toes. Your cursed words didn't just flow from your mouth; they flowed from your heart. Even when you decided to stop using profanity, you likely found yourself cursing anytime someone scared you or you hurt yourself. That's because those profane words were still in your heart, despite your best efforts to stop cursing. At the same time, when you gave your whole heart to GOD, and you began to subject yourself to the WORD of GOD consistently, you likely noticed a change in your words when you

The Power of Faith

hurt yourself or someone scared you. That's because a renewed mind will always make itself known in our speech as well as our choices.

As you read the Bible, you'll notice that the word "faith" is mentioned numerous times. In the King James version of the Bible, the word "faith" was mentioned two times in the Old Testament and it was mentioned 245 times in the New Testament. Why is this? That's because the shedding of CHRIST'S blood gave us the opportunity to be reconciled to GOD, but only through faith; meaning, we have to believe that CHRIST is the Son of GOD, HE died for our sins, and HE rose on the third day. In having faith in the WORD of GOD, we now have access to salvation, but again, we must believe it to receive it. In the Old Testament, the Jews had to follow a series of laws and rituals, but we no longer have to perform for GOD; we simply need faith.

Why is faith so important? Faith is the very foundation in which our relationship with GOD stands. Again, it is to trust in GOD and believe every WORD spoken by HIM. Without trust, there is no relationship. Think about a marriage. What if you were married and your spouse told you that he or she didn't trust you? Your marriage would undoubtedly go downhill after that confession because a person who does not trust you cannot be trusted. Additionally, a person who does not trust you cannot truly and wholly love you because to love you, they have to know you. If they don't trust you, they are saying that they don't know you; they only know what you've told them, and that's come under question.

The same goes with GOD. If you do not trust HIM, you do not truly know HIM, and if you don't know HIM, you can't love HIM. You can open your mouth and declare your love for HIM, but the truth will always be made evident in your decisions. For example, we like to say, *"Actions speak louder than words."* In other words, we are saying that what a person does will overshadow what they say because anyone who has a brain, a voice, and muscles around their mouths can form any words they choose to form. It's not uncommon for man to be liars; therefore, we know not to trust every word that comes out of a person's mouth. But we will watch what they do and draw a conclusion based on their actions.

→ **John 14:15:** If you love me, keep my

commandments.

Consider when JESUS questioned Peter repeatedly in the twenty-first book of John. When JESUS asked Peter for the third time if he loved HIM, the Bible tells us that Peter was grieved. This grief undoubtedly came about because Peter was worried that the LORD didn't believe that he loved HIM. To Peter, this repeated line of questioning may have caused him to feel that the LORD did not trust him. Each time that the LORD asked Peter if he loved HIM, HE gave HIM a commandment.

"So when they had dined, Jesus saith to Simon Peter, Simon, son of Jonas, lovest thou me more than these?
He saith unto him, Yea, Lord; thou knowest that I love thee.
He saith unto him, Feed my lambs.
He saith to him again the second time, Simon, son of Jonas, lovest thou me?
He saith unto him, Yea, Lord; thou knowest that I love thee.
He saith unto him, Feed my sheep.
He saith unto him the third time, Simon, son of Jonas, lovest thou me?

The Power of Faith

Peter was grieved because he said unto him the third time, Lovest thou me?
And he said unto him, Lord, thou knowest all things; thou knowest that I love thee.
Jesus saith unto him, Feed my sheep" *(John 21:15-17).*

CHRIST was saying to Peter that if he loved HIM, he'd feed HIS sheep, or basically, continue spreading the gospel of JESUS CHRIST. This takes us back to John 14:15 where the LORD says, *"If you love me, keep my commandments."* The keeping of the commandments isn't something that GOD is telling us we should consider doing; HE is and was saying that our choices will reveal how we truly feel about HIM. If we love HIM, we will keep HIS commandments. It's similar to what we say to our romantic interests. We'd say, "If you love me, you won't do this" or "If you love me, you will do that." If that person does something we've asked them not to do, it makes us question their love for us, and when we doubt their love, we doubt every word they've ever said to us.

One cannot love a GOD he does not trust or have faith in. For this reason, we ought to build our faith daily. That's why when teaching the Disciples to pray, CHRIST told them to say, *"Give us each day our daily bread."* JESUS is the Bread of Life, for HE is the living WORD of GOD.

Faith can literally move mountains. Faith can literally stop a storm. In the Bible, we've read about countless acts of faith that yielded some of the greatest victories known to man. We can also see demonstrations of faith in the earth today if we are involved in the faith circuit. Faith is the power of GOD being activated through a person because of that person's beliefs.

To affect a change in our mind, we must first introduce new information to ourselves and accept that information as truth, and this isn't always easy to do. Our minds are like courtrooms, and our hearts are the judges and jury behind every decision we make. Anytime something or someone is in our heart, we've allowed them there because of something we've believed. Sometimes our beliefs stem from what we have perceived about a situation or person, while other times, our beliefs stem from what we've been told about a situation or person. Let's say that you have a friend, and that friend has been in your life for

The Power of Faith

five years. Suddenly, that friend begins to behave strangely, and their behavior has raised some questions in your mind. In believing that they are behaving strangely, you are indicating that they are behaving contrary to their character, and this means that either their minds have changed or they're hiding something from you. For a few months, the friend who once called you everyday has changed her mind and now calls you once a week. When you answer her calls or when you call her, the conversations are short and you don't hear the characteristics of the person you once called "friend" in her voice. Now, your friendship is in the courts of your mind, and you are taking everything that has happened and is happening in as clues. Your love and familiarity with your friend will act as a lawyer in defense of your friendship, and that part of you will take into consideration every new event your friend has been through and how many years the two of you have been friends. But the recent character who's emerged in your friend will be the number one character witness for the Prosecutor: your heart. During the trial, you will likely pay closer attention to your friend's behavior, and you will question that friend more about their change of hearts. Finally, you will deliver your

The Power of Faith

verdict: Either your friend is guilty of betrayal (in your mind) or your friend is not guilty. To keep a friend around, you will have had to come to the conclusion that something changed in her life that's affecting a change in her thinking. If the events that have caused her to change are traumatic, you'll likely write her change of mind off as temporary. If the events that caused her to change her mind are a series of good events, you'll likely declare her guilty of betrayal and you'll begin the process of evicting her from your heart and life. Of course, ending a friendship or relationship is hurtful because anytime we let someone in our hearts, we make decisions based on them being in our lives. Letting go of them means letting go of the plans we've made with them. So, if your best friend is a single mother of three children, you'll likely center your future plans with her around her children. If you decide to disassociate from that friend, every plan you've built your life on will be torn down, and a season of uncertainty will replace your old plans; that is, until you've made new plans.

One of the remarkable things about faith is that it allows us to access the very blessings of GOD. We can have anything we ask for as long as we believe

The Power of Faith

GOD for it. The challenge that we oftentimes face is old beliefs that emerge to challenge new beliefs. What's amazing is that human beings aren't that great at guarding their hearts from the many lies floating around, but a liar or a person full of lies will guard his heart from the truth with the fierceness of a lioness guarding her cubs. Because we guard our hearts from the truth, it is difficult for us to embrace faith since we keep rejecting the truth. We can't have faith and lies dwelling in the same place; otherwise, we'll have faith in the wrong things.

If you want a new car, it's just a belief away. You get to set the terms of the agreement, but to do so, you are required to have faith the size of a mustard seed. Again, to have faith is to be consistently unchangeable. That means: No matter what situation comes forward to tell you that you cannot afford a new car, your faith in GOD has to remain consistent despite what you see. If your faith isn't consistent, you lose the right to set the terms of getting your new car, and the dealer then exercises his or her right to sell you the car on their own terms. You'll find many people in bondage to car notes today because they didn't have enough faith to set their own terms.

The Power of Faith

Your faith is your bank account, and Heaven is your account holder. Of course, GOD is the Owner and Founder of your banking institution, and HE has left an inheritance for you that has no limitations outside of what's in HIS will for you. This means that anything GOD has called good is accessible to you; only, you cannot covet, steal, or take anything that belongs to someone else. For example, GOD hates a divorce; therefore, you cannot pray to take the spouse of someone else. If you see someone with a car, house, or life you think you deserve, you are in error and you cannot bring such thinking before GOD and expect HIM to honor it, seeing as it is against HIM.

Whatever amount of faith you have, that's the amount of Heaven you get to bring down and earth you get to take up. If you walk onto a land that's for sale and believe GOD for that land, that land is your land, but again, you can only inherit it if your faith does not waiver. The very minute you ask GOD for something, the enemy launches an attack against your prayer. That's why it's good to pray in the Spirit daily. If the enemy can hear your prayers, he will do everything that he can to stop you from believing GOD. The reason he launches an attack against your belief system is because out of the abundance of your heart, your mouth will speak. At the same time, whatever you believe, you will receive. In other words, by getting you to doubt GOD, he can challenge the trust you have in GOD, thus challenging your relationship with GOD altogether. Below is a parable that CHRIST spoke to a crowd that was gathered, and the interpretation of that parable that HE gave to HIS Disciples.

> → **Mark 4:2-9:** And he taught them many things by parables, and said unto them in his doctrine, Hearken; Behold, there went out a sower to sow: And it came to pass, as he sowed, some fell by the way side, and the fowls of the air came and devoured it up. And some fell on stony ground, where it had not much earth; and immediately it sprang up, because it had no depth of earth: But when the sun was up, it was scorched; and because it had no root, it withered away. And some fell among thorns, and the thorns grew up, and choked it, and it yielded no fruit. And other fell on good ground, and did yield fruit that sprang up and increased; and brought forth, some thirty, and

some sixty, and some an hundred. And he said unto them, He that hath ears to hear, let him hear.

→ **Mark 4:14:20:** The sower soweth the word. And these are they by the way side, where the word is sown; but when they have heard, Satan cometh immediately, and taketh away the word that was sown in their hearts. And these are they likewise which are sown on stony ground; who, when they have heard the word, immediately receive it with gladness; And have no root in themselves, and so endure but for a time: afterward, when affliction or persecution ariseth for the word's sake, immediately they are offended. And these are they which are sown among thorns; such as hear the word, And the cares of this world, and the deceitfulness of riches, and the lusts of other things entering in, choke the word, and it becometh unfruitful. And these are they which are sown on good ground; such as hear the word, and receive it, and bring forth fruit, some thirtyfold, some sixty, and some an hundred.

In Mark 4, the LORD demonstrated to us just how the

enemy works against our faith. HE said that when the sower sows the WORD, Satan comes **immediately** to uproot the WORD. The enemy doesn't tarry or delay in coming against what you've been praying or believing GOD for. GOD said that people who have no root or depth receive the WORD with gladness, but because they have no depth in the WORD, the cares of this world choke the WORD and it becomes unfruitful; meaning, they will not receive what they've been praying for. For this reason, many of us have prayed for things and have not seen the manifestation of what we've been praying for. When we don't receive what we've been praying for, the little faith that we do have begins to point in the opposite direction, and this causes us to have more faith in ourselves than GOD. But the error was not in GOD; the error was allowing the cares of the world to choke the WORD out of us.

The scriptures go on to say that the WORD, when sown on good ground, brings forth good fruit. The measure of fruit that we bring forth depends on the measure of faith in which we have. That's why it is important to read and meditate on the WORD of GOD daily. The more WORD you have in you, the more faith you'll have access to, and this will give you

The Power of Faith

access to GOD'S yeas and amen.

> → **Hebrews 11:6:** But without faith it is impossible to please him: for he that cometh to God must believe that he is, and that he is a rewarder of them that diligently seek him.

Without faith it is impossible to please GOD. Most people read this religiously, and give no heed to this warning because it is human nature to think that a little reasoning could change someone's mind. Many believers today think they are "good enough" to change GOD'S mind. They consider their good deeds and they mentally frame the sacrifices they've made for GOD, thus making light of the sacrifices HE has made for them. Many believers stay in sin, and quote the all-too-popular cliché, *"GOD knows my heart."* Nevertheless, without faith, the Bible tells us that it is **impossible** to please GOD. How can one get faith? *"So then faith cometh by hearing, and hearing by the word of God" (Romans 10:17).*

Faith isn't something we can just wake up and claim; faith has to be ushered in by the WORD of GOD. Where there is no WORD, there is no faith. Where

The Power of Faith

there is little WORD, there is little faith. Many believers today memorize the scriptures that have become somewhat of a motto for their churches. They hear their pastors saying these scriptures repeatedly, and they eventually learn those particular scriptures by heart. Because of this, many believers only have as much WORD as man gives them, and even though they have Bibles at home, their Bibles collect dust during the week. It isn't until their regularly scheduled church services or Bible studies that their Bibles are dusted off and opened.

Faith is the power to receive supernatural things. It is one's ability to connect with GOD, beyond our earthly understandings, and to exercise the supernatural power of GOD in the natural realm. With faith, you not only please GOD, but you get to tap into Heaven itself. With faith, no good thing is withheld from you. In faith, nothing by shall any means harm you. By faith, the brokenhearted are healed, the mute speak, the lame walk, the blind see, and the dead arise to live again. When you have faith, nothing can successfully stand against you. It can stand up, but faith will always bring it down. To live, walk, and speak in faith is to be in total agreement with GOD. Please

The Power of Faith

remember that HIS WORD has never, will never, and can never return to HIM void. The earth and everything in it belongs to GOD, and has to move at the sound of HIS voice. Everything in the realm of the earth absolutely has to obey GOD. So, when you believe GOD for whatever it is you are believing HIM for, you are in the same coming in agreement with HIM. With or without your agreement, HIS WORD will stand, but when you come in agreement with HIS WORD, you get to stand on the blessed side of HIS WORD. Of all the things you can have in the realm of the earth, faith is the most valuable possession, for it gives you access to everything GOD has access to.

Fear: The Boa Constrictor of Faith

The house erupted in laughter as my younger sister limped through the front door. Just moments earlier, we'd heard her screaming "wasp" repeatedly. She'd finally arrived to the safety nest of the house. She was covered in grass and holding her abdomen as she limped towards the couch. Trying to restrain my laughter, I listened as she explained to my mother and I that a wasp had tried to land on her, so she panicked and tried to run away. She tripped over some object and fell to the ground. According to some neighbors, she'd flipped before hitting the ground while trying to get away from the wasp. "Did it sting you?" I chuckled "No," she said. "I got away from it." I looked at my sister once again. Her hair was disheveled from the fall and fragments of grass hung in her hair and stuck to her clothes like tree ornaments. She had a few scrapes and bruises from the fall, and she was observing the fresh wound on one of her knees. "You know. You did far more damage to yourself than that wasp would have done to you," I said before erupting in laughter once again.

Fear: The Boa Constrictor of Faith

We'd grown up to fear wasps because my mother feared wasps. We feared wasps so much that we often hurt ourselves trying to get away from them. In fearing wasps, we were acknowledging the power that they possessed, and this, of course, was the power to sting us.

Whatever you fear, you reverence; meaning, you respect the authority of it. When you fear something, it begins to erect itself in a godlike fashion in your heart, and that's why GOD commands that we fear nothing and no person but HIMSELF. Fear is a reaction to whatever you believe is going to happen to you. Because you believe something will happen, you will find ways to make sacrifices to avoid being overtaken by the thing in which you fear. For example, if you were walking to the store, but feared a few loiterers who hung out on the short route to the store, you'll likely take the long route. The sacrifice you made trying to avoid the loiterers was the time and energy you spent taking the long route.

Whatever you fear, you will make sacrifices to. Again, fear is a form of reverence, and anything you reverence begins to become godlike in your heart.

Fear: The Boa Constrictor of Faith

I can remember going out with my mother to hang clothes on the clothesline when I was a young girl. I hated hanging clothes out because there were always wasps living in the poles that held up the lines. We'd always start hanging clothes from the middle of the line and make our way towards the poles. We would often go in opposite directions, and my mother would hang clothes on one of the lines while I hung clothes on the other line. Then, it would happen. I'd hear her screaming and see her running in my direction. She'd suddenly grab me and hold me in front of her. I would scream, wriggle my way out of her hands and we'd both run into the house. I didn't notice this pattern until I became a teenager. I was about fifteen years old, and we were following our normal pattern of hanging clothes. Both of us were nearing the poles on each opposite end when suddenly, I heard my mother scream and I saw her looking in my direction; meaning, she was about to come my way. I laughed and ran in the opposite direction as she pursued me screaming for me to wait up. I didn't wait. I kept running and I kept laughing.

After we were in the house, I jokingly brought it to her attention. "You always try to use me as a sacrifice for

Fear: The Boa Constrictor of Faith

the wasps," I said. Not realizing that she'd been doing that, my mother laughingly questioned my words, and I brought it to her attention. "Ever since I was young, you would always pick me up and hold me in front of you anytime you saw a wasp or a bee. You're basically saying, 'Here's my daughter. Sting her, not me.'" My mother apologized and we laughed about the event, but I knew then that if there was a wasp or a bee within a few feet of my mother, I was to always run in the opposite direction.

I was my mother's sacrifice. In exchange for her not being bitten, she offered me as an alternative. Of course, I wouldn't have died because I'm not allergic to bee or wasp stings, but I would have had to endure the pain from the stings of those wasps. And she didn't realize what she was doing; she was simply reacting out of fear. After all, whatever you fear, you will offer a sacrifice to, and sacrifices aren't necessarily giving the life of something or someone you love; it's giving up something you ordinarily wouldn't give up in exchange for something you want. For example, when I decided to lose weight, I had to make a sacrifice. I had to give up many of the foods I'd come to love in exchange for a smaller waistline.

Fear: The Boa Constrictor of Faith

Ordinarily, I wouldn't give up those foods, but I had to give them up if I wanted to be smaller.

Fear is like a high definition simulator. It offers you the controls while the enemy shows you the scary alternatives to GOD'S declarations. You find yourself emotionally navigating through your imaginations, fearful of the obstacles ahead. The WORD tells you to be still and know that JEHOVAH is GOD, but fear will make you move. While in fear, you will attempt to avoid all of the pits ahead; all the while, keeping your eyes focused on whatever destination you want to arrive at. Fear makes you go back under the law in which CHRIST delivered you from because you'll begin to trust in your own works, understanding and strength, rather than trusting in GOD.

Fear is the boa constrictor of faith. It squeezes our faith until unbelief pops out. What exactly is a boa constrictor? A boa constrictor is a large snake native to North America and recognized by its large markings and pinkish or tan coloring. Boa constrictors are nocturnal snakes, rarely coming out in the daytime. A boa kills its prey through asphyxiation by wrapping its body around the animal and squeezing it

Fear: The Boa Constrictor of Faith

to death. Every time the prey breathes, the snake tightens its grip until its prey can no longer breathe.

That's how fear works. It coils itself around whatever you've believed GOD for, and it squeezes the life out of your faith. You see, faith is an incubator that allows whatever you've been asking GOD for to develop and live. Fear cuts off the power to that incubator, thus, killing your faith and anything in its womb. After disbelief arises, you will continue to speak religiously; attempting to speak life into whatever you've believed GOD for, and hoping that your religious words are enough to revive your faith, but it's not. You would have to start the process all over again, asking GOD for whatever it is you want to ask HIM for, and then, protecting your faith's incubator from any thoughts or manifestations that threaten it. You protect your prayers by building your faith. How do you build your faith? Romans 10:1 gives us the answer: *"So then faith cometh by hearing, and hearing by the word of God."*

To get faith, we must hear the WORD of GOD. Think about a time when your life seemed irreparable. You'd pretty much resigned yourself to the very fate in which

Fear: The Boa Constrictor of Faith

you'd feared, and you'd began preparing your life for the impact you were anticipating. While waiting, you decided to go to church, and it was one of the best decisions you could have made. While the pastor was teaching, you felt revived and your faith was restored. You left the sanctuary anxious and ready to apply whatever you'd just learned. What happened was the pastor breathed life into your faith, and you felt strong enough to fight that constrictor that had wrapped itself around your faith. You simply changed your mind. You stopped seeing defeat as inevitable and you started fighting back, unraveling that doubt that had been coiled around your belief system. Suddenly, you had the strength to go on; suddenly, you had hope. When an animal is dying and it gives up hope, that animal will no longer fight death. It will resign itself to death, hoping that the process will be swift and painless. An animal that has hope in it will be a predator's nightmare because that animal will fight back, and many times, an animal that looks as if it is as good as dead, will find the strength to free itself and flee its would-be killer. That's because it did not lose hope, despite the odds against it.

What odds are against you? The truth is, GOD gets

Fear: The Boa Constrictor of Faith

the most glory from the most hopeless looking situations, so even when you're going through a hard spot, just remember that GOD wants the glory.

Like the boa constrictor, fear finds its nest in our darkest hours. It hides behind our fake smiles and empty words. It strikes when we get within its range, searching our minds and hearts for answers other than the WORD of GOD. It wraps itself around our thoughts and tightens its grip every time we breathe out another complaint or doubt. Finally, there's no life left in our hopes and beliefs, and we resolve ourselves to doing the work we believe to be necessary to acquire what we'd initially prayed for.

Faith opposes fear and fear walks in opposition of faith; therefore, both faith and fear cannot play for the same team. Again, to overcome fear, you need faith; and to get faith, you need to hear the WORD.

Deceptive Perception

Perception. Oh, what an ugly word perception can be. I can't count the amount of times I've stood frozen, staring down the barrel of someone's perception of who I was, who I should be, or who I should have become. By the time I was an adult, I'd learned to dodge perception's bullets because I came to understand that perception was a powerless weapon yielded by people who are led by jealousy, a sense of entitlement, or a combination of both. Neither of those things can harm you if you don't let it.

When I failed at something, and my reality wasn't looking so good, I was liked.... *really liked*. Many familiar faces offered me their support, their love, and anything else I needed. As a matter of fact, when I was going through my first divorce, I was surprised at how the people who'd once kept their distances from me were suddenly interested in being a part of my life again. They wanted to know what happened in my marriage, and what I'd been up to over the years. They wanted to see if their expectations of me had

Deceptive Perception

proven true or were still in development. Suddenly, I had an audience (lynch mob) gathering to see my dramatic ending. They were a friendly bunch of vultures, but I wasn't in the least bit surprised or moved by their seemingly kind gestures because I knew them well. I simply reciprocated with a smile, but I kept my eyes open because I knew who and what I was dealing with.

Make-believing that they were there for me helped me treat them with the love and respect the LORD wanted me to treat them with. Truthfully, there were times when I'd almost fooled myself into believing that they had actually changed for the better; after all, most of them were family members, but like always, my life began to take a turn for the better, and the crowd began to disperse and complain. Like always, I found myself staring down the barrels of their perception, a perception that GOD had proven to be wrong many times.

Perception is the enemy's version of discernment. It is man's understanding in the form of an opinion. Now, there is Godly discernment, and there is perception, and of course, there's a fine line between the two.

Deceptive Perception

Godly discernment comes from GOD and what HE has taught us, and is used to protect us from others who may not have our best interests in mind. Perception comes from our understandings, and our understandings are based on our experiences, the conditions of our hearts and whatever forces we're struggling with. You'll know the difference between the two when you examine the fruit of the two. Perception is oftentimes selfish. Many people who throw perception around do so with the intent of befriending or getting something from the people they are attempting to label. But those labels can't stick unless the person they're being applied to believes they are who the perceiving one says they are. For this reason, when you don't accept someone's perception of you, they'll become offended because they have ulterior motives. Godly discernment is selfless and is used by GOD to show us how to minister to the people we're communicating it. People with Godly discernment won't usually stick around in your life to see if their labels stick, but people who lean to their own understandings will always want front row seats to your life. That's because they want to see if their perception is truly discernment or prophetic.

Deceptive Perception

People who often label others do so because of the hurt within themselves. The labels they hand out are designed to position people in their lives according to what they feel they need. In other words, their perception is selfishly motivated to chisel people into the characters they want in their lives. What they are saying is that the positions they have open in their lives require you to be one way, but since you are currently another way, they need to break you, build you back up, and to train you for those roles in their lives. So, they'll fire off a list of things they perceive to be wrong with you; things they believe would pose as an obstacle to their plans for you. If you're not the type of person who cares about what others think of you, they may attribute that characteristic as a character flaw if they're used to controlling the people around them with their opinions. If you're not broken, but everyone currently in their lives are broken and dependent upon their opinions, they may attempt to look for any unhealed wounds in you. When they can't find any, they'll tell you that you have those wounds anyway. Again, the goal is to get you to fit into their perceptions and their plans, even if that means bringing you outside of GOD'S will for yourself.

Deceptive Perception

Perception can be deadly to both the person yielding it and the people it's being thrown at because perception is a Satanic dart designed to change one's reality by changing their minds. The person who wrongfully perceives another person is attempting to erect him or herself as a needed force in that person's life. In other words, they began to unknowingly and foolishly erect themselves as idols, and this behavior is dangerous.

The enemy is going to look to change your mind. He's going to send lost souls your way, and those souls will come from varying walks of life and faith. Some of those souls will be downright mean-spirited, while others will be seemingly harmless. Some of those souls will be people who have no rapport with you, while others will be people you truly love and respect. And they'll begin to unload their perception of you on you whenever they feel that they have the clearest shot at your heart. The point is that you need to be ready for every dart the enemy is going to throw at you. All too often, believers are turned back to the wildernesses that GOD had called them out of simply because of another believer's perception of them. You need to be prepared for what is to come if you intend

Deceptive Perception

to go all the way in CHRIST. You have to make up your mind that you will not turn back, regardless of what happens, who walks out of your life, and whatever you're confronted with. At the same time, be careful that you don't spitefully use others for your own advancement. Know this: The entire time you are looking to others to help you achieve your goals, you will have taken your eyes off GOD. What you'll find is that when you simply trust GOD and do whatever HE told you to do, you will continue to advance forward, and you will advance a lot faster than the people around you who are depending on other people.

Can you handle the backlash associated with change? What human being or situation has enough power in your life to turn you back into your wilderness? Identify whomever or whatever is in your life that has enough power to move you, and then, bring that potential issue before the LORD before it becomes an actual issue. If you have friends in your life that the LORD has told you to let go of, go ahead and release them. If you have family members in your life that the LORD has told you to disconnect from, go ahead and unplug yourself from them. Whatever it is that GOD told you to do, do it. Don't you dare allow

Deceptive Perception

yourself to be turned back into your old mindset because of someone's perception of you. Many of the people who will speak evil of you already have evil in their hearts for you, but they hide it behind a smile and a few kind words. If you want to really see how someone feels about you, step outside of what you know and let God promote you. They will either tell you or show you how they truly feel about you during your promotion or after it. Some people will never tell you how they perceive you; instead, they'll tell individuals who are closest to you because they want to find a handle on your life using those people. But let those who will fall away fall away. Let those who will judge you be judged by the very judgments they sent out for you. Let those who wrongfully perceive you live with their own perceptions, because their perceptions are their own deceptions, not yours. How someone feels about you is absolutely none of your business. That's between them and the LORD. Your job is to obey GOD and get past any and every obstacle that the enemy places on your path, with one of those greatest obstacles being human emotions and perceptions. Sadly enough, many have turned away from GOD and went back into those dry places HE'S called them out of. They have rejected their

Deceptive Perception

callings for the sake of pleasing a bunch of people who were outside of the will of GOD and can't stand to see anyone who is in it.

Defining Moments

In life, there are moments that we freeze in our minds, and we store them away in our hearts as keepsakes. These moments are what we refer to as defining moments. Defining moments are those occurrences when time seemed to have stood still and we were invited into or forced into a change. After each defining moment, our perceptions were changed and our lives were changed. Defining moments include the birth of a child, marriage, divorce, betrayal, revelations (good or bad), economic shifts, and so on.

It goes without saying that a lot of people have allowed pain to define them. There were instances in time where they were hurt so badly that they were forced into change, and the changes they were forced into were less than favorable conditions. Having endured and overcome the adversities they'd faced, many have barricaded themselves in behind their fears. They don't allow a lot of people in their lives, and anyone who attempts to walk away from them is dramatically and violently opposed. That's because

Defining Moments

they are still responding to the pain they've endured over the courses of their lives. Their pain has defined them.

There are also people out who have allowed themselves to be defined by their wealth. Anytime we are shifted economically, we must be prepared spiritually and mentally for the shift; otherwise, we would enter new realms with old understandings, and this can be dangerous. Consider the all-too-common stories of husbands leaving their wives after suddenly coming into large amounts of money. With more money comes more opportunities, and these husbands wanted to seize every opportunity that was availed to them. In these stories, the common ending is: The husband marries another woman; namely, his money-loving mistress. The mistress has one or two kids with him before leaving him and taking half of his assets with her. She also ruins him financially, socially, and emotionally. The now bitter ex-husband takes on a new sport: drinking and gambling. By the time he's sixty years old, he's a shell of what he once was, and he passes away, having become nothing more than a byword to those who once knew him. We all know this story, and many of us know someone

Defining Moments

who fits this description. His defining moment was the day he was granted access to wealth that he obviously didn't have the wisdom to hold. Wealth without wisdom is dangerous; it is a stronghold that has imprisoned many shallow men and women.

Your life today is like a building, and everything that's ever happened to you is a part of your building. You've either made it a part of the building or a part of the design.
Whatever you have made a part of the building will determine if and how long that building stands. Whatever you have made a part of the design of that building will determine how you perceive yourself and others. When you forgive those who have trespassed against you, you make them a part of the design; meaning, you frame those moments to be nothing more than lessons to teach others by. When you don't forgive those who have trespassed against you, you make them a part of the building; meaning, many (if not all) of your life's choices are based on or motivated by what they've done to you.

Every decision you have ever made and every choice that you will make was and is motivated by those

Defining Moments

defining moments in your life. For example, if your parents told you that they were proud of the person you were becoming, that would likely be a defining moment in your life; a moment where you were motivated to change your life and work harder at making your parents proud. Many adults today went to college and earned advanced degrees because of those emotionally charged moments when their parents expressed their approval of them. At the same time, many adults today have gone to prison and gotten lengthy sentences because of an emotionally charged moment (or series of moments) when their parents expressed their disappointment in them. It goes without saying, however, that we can't continue to blame our parents for our shortcomings.

The enemy is always looking for an opportunity to create another defining moment in your life; a moment where your faith is shattered, your fears are realized, and new doubts are established. For this reason, the enemy works tirelessly to station people around you who are not sold out for CHRIST. These people see something in you that they want, and they often have something in themselves that you feel you need. Many friendships are centered around co-dependency

Defining Moments

and established because of voids. When the enemy successfully stations someone in your life, that person's job is to season you for the enemy so that he can devour you. They'll hurt you, ridicule you, mislead you, spitefully use you, and repeatedly mishandle you until you become bitter, vengeful, and distrusting. From there, you begin to think in a manner that goes against GOD, and this is when the enemy begins to devour his prey. Of course, you shouldn't let the pain define you, but it goes without saying that many believers have created lives and ministries based on their pain.

Defining moments are often refining moments. If you think back, you'll notice that most of the major changes in your thinking and your life started with a traumatic event. If you have asked GOD for the wisdom in those traumatic events, HE will give you understanding, but if you've tried to define those moments based on how you felt, those moments have begun to define you. Of course, most people don't think to ask GOD to define what they'd just endured; instead, most people look at the problem, draft up a conclusion, and attempt to find a solution. This means that, as human beings, most of us see the outside or

Defining Moments

the manifestation of what we've been through, but we don't see the roots of those issues. For this reason, the same situations and problems become familiar recurrences in our lives until we finally submit to a peculiar GOD.

Be careful what and who you allow to define you. Believe it or not, more than half of the people walking the earth have allowed some situation or a series of situations define them. For example, there are some young adults who were preparing to go to college when they were suddenly offered well-paying jobs. The prospect of college suddenly began to lose its appeal; especially, for those children who thought they were in love. They allowed the idea of getting a job and wearing the label associated with their jobs to define them. Thirty years later, they are still wearing that same name badge that was handed to them three decades ago.

I was one of those people....for a while. My first job was at Wal-Mart, and I decided to put college off because I allowed a car note to bully me. I didn't want to lose my car, and I was too afraid to commute back and forth to college, so I delayed the idea of going to

Defining Moments

college. Seven years later, I finally walked away from Wal-Mart, surprised at the amount of people who were sucked into the idea of earning barely enough wages to survive with; people who'd somehow allowed themselves to be defined by their jobs. I met so many wonderful people while employed at Wal-Mart, and they didn't believe they could ever do anything outside of what they were doing; after all, many of them didn't have college degrees. I have never went to college, but GOD still used me for HIS glory.

I remember going to some co-workers one day and telling them that we ought to start looking for better paying jobs or start our own businesses. I was convinced that we were worth far more than we were getting paid.
I was young, ambitious, and there was a drive in me to do something with my life; a drive in which I did not understand at that time. One of the women giggled as she turned to address my sudden outburst. She laughed as she told me that I was still young and didn't have children yet; therefore, I didn't understand life. She told me that a lot of companies close their doors, leaving their employees without jobs, but she

Defining Moments

assured me that Wal-Mart would always be around. She said that if she stayed with Wal-Mart, she knew she'd always have a job.

What happened with her and many of the wonderful, talented people who'd given Wal-Mart and other low-paying jobs thirty and forty years of their lives? They allowed themselves to be defined by life, cornered by fear, and complacent with whatever was given to them. Now, that's not to say that everyone who works for Wal-Mart or any other retail chain isn't happy with their jobs. There are many people who work for Wal-Mart and companies like Wal-Mart, and they are happy with their jobs, but having worked in retail for seven years, I can safely say that more than ninety percent of the people who make a career out of low-paying jobs do so out of fear. They don't see themselves as intelligent; they don't see themselves as being able to do more than what they are already doing. They fear change; they fear the unforeseeable, and because of their fears, they settle for just enough to make a living with.

Additionally, there are people, companies, and ministries that lock people behind their doors by

Defining Moments

offering them positions in leadership. Sometimes, we don't know just how blessed and anointed we are, but others can see what we are blind to. Because of this, many anointed souls walk into ministries to sit amongst the congregation and be fed the WORD of GOD, and they walk out having been given some position in that ministry. Quite naturally, they are excited at the prospect of working with a ministry, so they accept the offer and give their all to their leaders. Years later, they begin to mature and their eyes suddenly begin to open, but they don't want to believe what they are seeing. They start operating in the anointing that GOD has placed on their lives, only to have the leaders of the ministries they've joined to try and control their anointings. They try to stay in those ministries, but betrayal and church hurt drives them to the reality that they are going to have to separate themselves from those ministries. The leaders of the ministries then begin attempting to speak word curses over them, saying these people are out of the will of GOD, and that something bad was going to happen to them. I've heard this type of story one too many times. I've spoken with members who'd separated themselves from ministries that had given them a position or ordained them not long after they'd entered

Defining Moments

that church building. I've spoken with leaders who thought it was okay to speak evil of the sheep whose souls they once watched over (or exposed).

The message here is: Many people will seek to give you defining moments in their attempts to define or redefine you. You may not know who you are and what you're called or chosen to do, but sometimes, the enemy does. It's human nature to want to excel at something, and if you've had your potential bottled up for a long time, any opportunity that looks superior to what you are doing may audition to be that defining moment in your life; that moment when you surrender everything GOD has called you to be so that you can be whatever or whomever someone else is calling you. When you don't know who you are, there will be plenty of people who will tell you who you should be or who they think you are. They'll define you according to their needs, and they'll pervert your walk by bringing you in subjection to themselves. When you're young and unlearned, you may think you're being elevated and given the opportunity of a lifetime, but the truth is: The enemy simply used a moment of joy to cause you to define yourself according to the opportunities that were before you at that time. Again, this is not uncommon. It happens very often, not just

Defining Moments

in the church, but also in life generally. For example, you may find yourself at a low place in your life, and suddenly, someone comes along and offers you their friendship. In that moment, they seem to be everything you need in a friend because you are attempting to define whatever you are going through or allowing your situation to define you. Like clockwork, your new friend is in your life, and offering you advice that goes against what you believe, but it appears to be good advice. They may tell you their stories of overcoming the very thing in which you are struggling with. What's happening in this moment is they are attempting to get you to redefine yourself by seeing the situation from their points of view. One easy way to tell if GOD sends them into your life is to simply refuse to do things their way. Just stay put and do what GOD told you to do. When a person can't define you, they'll redefine the terms of their friendship with you. It won't be long before they separate themselves from you. *"Submit yourselves therefore to God. Resist the devil, and he will flee from you"* *(James 4:7).*

Additionally, one of the worst things that can happen to a person is that they get a worldly promotion

Defining Moments

without GOD'S permission. Wherever you are when you are promoted, you are likely to get locked into that mindset. Wealth without wisdom is a snare. When a man imagines a vain thing, he visits a place he doesn't have GOD'S permission to enter. That's why our imaginations have to be managed by the WORD of GOD daily. Consider the young boy who knows how to dance well. He watched a lot of television, and while other boys his age were playing video games, he was teaching himself how to dance. Suddenly, he's entered into a competition, and he wins. He begins to ascend the ranks of entertainment, and now, he's defined by what he can do, not who he is scheduled to become. Dancing is something he's learned to do, but it's necessarily his identity.

He spends years dancing for what he believes to be his loyal fans, but one day, another young man comes out and he's a better dancer. Suddenly, that little boy who was once celebrated by the masses is nothing more than a vague memory, and he learns just how disloyal his estranged fans are. His money is soon depleted, and he can't imagine getting a job. After all, society defined him as a dancer, so he accepted their definition of who he was and he attempted to become that. Years later, he's depressed, suicidal, and trying

Defining Moments

hard to be reconciled to the people who once defined him. He wants to outshine his competition and prove himself to be worthy of their praises. But he's washed up, and his body can no longer keep up with his mind. One day, he goes home and takes his own life.

Why did he kill himself? It's simple: He didn't know GOD; therefore, he didn't know who he was. Our identities are wrapped up in GOD, and we can't know who we truly are until we approach the Throne of GOD and receive our identities from the FATHER. In the meantime, we will wear many personalities as we attempt to define ourselves, and we'll search for those defining moments that appear to uncover the answers to every question we've ever had.

Get a pen and paper out, and write down those defining moments in your life, and note how each of those moments have caused major changes in your life. If you haven't forgiven someone, choose to forgive them and lay the problem at the altar so that it can no longer be a problem for you. If you find that some occurrence has sent you down the wrong roads in life and led you to make some pretty bad choices, take that occurrence and lay it on the altar of GOD.

Defining Moments

Your life will never change until your mind changes. Once you lay everything that has defined you on the altar of GOD, and you leave it there, you'll begin to redefine who you are based on what GOD reveals to you about who HE has created you to be. If you lay a mentality or problem on the altar during prayer, and you find yourself picking it back up again, take it back to the altar and lay it at the feet of GOD again. Keep doing this until you finally release it for good. Each defining moment in our lives is wisdom-packed and knowledge-filled, and if we don't allow those moments to define us, GOD will give us the understanding we need to define those moments.

Mental Inversion

I was heading to the checkouts at my local Super Wal-Mart one day when the LORD spoke to my heart. HE told me to look at the people around me, and HE showed me how what was on the inside of them was made evident by the clothes they chose to wear. Sure, the old cliché says that one cannot judge a book by its cover, but truthfully, you can get an idea as to what the book is about by looking at the cover. You may not get the full story, but you can get an idea. I saw people who were fully covered and seemingly respectable, and I also saw half-dressed characters, tattoo covered characters, and men whose pants draped underneath their derrieres. I considered the time I'd gone to a local J.C. Penny and saw a man covered with tattoos. He had a shaved head and looked like my idea of a racist, biker gang affiliate, but to my surprise, when he spoke, he spoke of JESUS CHRIST. That is to say that some people do get saved after they've permanently altered their appearances; nevertheless, most people don't change their minds as they get older. They simply join into new fads.

As I neared the checkout, a woman passed me by wearing an extremely revealing tank top. The way she walked spoke volumes about her character. She opened her mouth and began to scream obscenities at one or more of her children. I was amazed at what I was witnessing. People wear their mentalities inside out.

Now, it's no secret that some people are really good at concealing their character, especially if they try to play into a certain role to achieve a goal. A person who intentionally deceives others by mimicking the clothing, personalities, and words of the character types they are trying to impress are oftentimes very crafty and dangerous. Even though dressed in what we consider to be normal clothing, such characters are wearing costumes.

> → **2 Corinthians 11:14:** And no marvel; for Satan himself is transformed into an angel of light.

Even though no good is found in Satan, the Bible tells us that he impersonates an angel of light, which of course, is an angel of GOD. Other Biblical translations state that he masquerades or disguises himself as an angel of light. This act is an attempt to deceive people who wouldn't follow him if he came dressed as himself.

Of course, we know that there are false teachers, apostles, and prophets on the loose, and most of these characters wear priestly robes. To the naked eye, they appear to be holy vessels of GOD, but they are ravenous wolves looking to deceive and destroy GOD'S people. Nowadays, false teachers don't have to wear costumes, because we live in a time where many believers are determined to have their sin while declaring their salvation. We live in a time where many are looking for bridges to bridge the gap between sin and righteousness, and for this reason, many false teachers are quickly ascending the ranks amongst men. To a church that refuses to divorce her sins, these teachers represent the lies Satan has been telling them. They've fought long and hard to keep their immoral lifestyles, and now people they can relate to have microphones, and these people are a representation of their lusts manifested. For a long time, they'd worn costumes trying to cover up who

Mental Inversion

they really were in an attempt to fool a church that they believed to be judgmental. But nowadays, ministers are raising up who look like the world, talk like the world, preach like the world, but have the wisdom of the church. To the blind, these worldly ministers represent the lies they've been telling themselves: They don't have to change their minds or their lives; they don't have to live holy after all. All they have to do is play church on Sunday mornings, and for the rest of the week, they can splurge in the sins they've grown to love. To the worldly-minded, believing woman, these ministers represent the worldly men they've secretly lusted after. They represent the sin these women have come to love so dearly, all wrapped up in a man who's representing CHRIST. It's easy to see that such men are ambitious lovers of self, but because so many women shun holiness, they are easily fooled when what they really need (the WORD of GOD) appears to be living in what they want (the sinner man). To the worldly-minded, believing man, such characters represent the lifestyles they want with the GOD they need. A false teacher is only successful amongst people who don't know the truth. *"Jesus saith unto him, I am the way, the truth, and the life: no man cometh unto the Father,*

Mental Inversion

but by me" (John 14:6).

Of course, as the hour draws nearer for the return of GOD, we will see an influx in false teachers, prophets, and apostles, and many of these characters will wear costumes when needed. After all, there are still people around who must see the appearance of holiness, even if holiness is not present amongst them. But for the ones who don't need the costume, the enemy will come dressed as himself and he will draw the people using the very lusts they refuse to get delivered from. Many are being imprisoned by the cares of this world, and only few are living for GOD in this hour. *"And because iniquity shall abound, the love of many shall wax cold" (Matthew 24:12).*

The average person wears his or her personality, characteristics, and beliefs on the outside. Just as we have unique faces that serve as identifying markers for others to recognize us, the garments and accessories we wear on the outside oftentimes serve as markers for others to identify our character. In every stage of my faith, what was on the inside of me manifested outwardly. There was a time when I was in the world wholly, and my mentality could be

Mental Inversion

seen in my choices of attire. If my clothing wasn't enough to bear witness to what was on the inside of me, my words were. Like most believers, I started going to church, but the love of GOD just wasn't in me yet, so I tried to cover up a little, but I still wore revealing clothes. Years would pass before I finally surrendered wholeheartedly to GOD, and as HIS WORD came to dwell in me, I found myself shopping for clothes that covered me. Even though I knew many scriptures over the years, I was still pretty much sold out for the world. I came to church and I desired to know GOD, but the world was what I knew; it was what I was familiar and comfortable with. Each new change of heart was made evident by a change in my attire.

When I was in the world, I'd come across many people who spoke of GOD, but I didn't trust them because their spirits were familiar to me. Having been broken and accustomed to dysfunctional thinking, it goes without saying that I was surrounded by familiar spirits. Because I'd spent my life around some pretty shady characters, it wasn't hard for me to recognize devils masquerading as saints. On one particular occasion, I was working when a friend of mine told me

Mental Inversion

that one of our co-workers wanted to borrow some money from her. I warned her not to give the money to that woman because I recognized the love of money in her. Of course, I didn't say I could see her love of money, even though she hid who she was behind a constant stream of "hallelujahs" and "praise GOD" quotes. I simply warned my friend, but she didn't listen, and she loaned her the money anyway. Again, my friend and I were in the world, and this woman was presenting herself as a woman of GOD. Needless to say, my friend never got the money back. She'd called the borrower's house, only to be told by her children that she wasn't at home. She'd visited her house, and even saw her peeking out of the blinds, only to have her not answer her door. She'd confronted her at work, only to have her repeatedly give excuses and new dates in which she was to come by and get her money. I didn't know it then, but I was operating in the gift of discernment. Just as people have identifying traits, spirits have identifying traits. Having been around the worst of the worst, I'd learned to identify certain spirits, even though I didn't know at that time that I was identifying the characteristics of demonic spirits. At the same time, when I came in contact with people who were really

Mental Inversion

sold out for the LORD, I marveled at them. They were foreign to me, and I was drawn to them. I wanted to understand what made them tick, and I wanted to hang out with them in hopes that they could help me to become a better person.

What about the thieving woman who'd deceived my friend? She covered herself the way a woman of the church would normally cover herself. She didn't wear revealing clothes, nor did she channel any seductive spirits that you'll commonly see in many believers and leaders today. She was well disguised, but I only recognized her spirit because I'd met it one too many times. That is to say that we won't always be able to tell the character of a person based on the clothes they are wearing, but if we ask GOD for discernment, we'll be able to look past the costumes to see the real devils underneath.

If you are still wearing revealing clothing, clothing that causes people to lust after you, now is not the time to say, "GOD knows my heart." Instead, it's a great time to ask GOD to review your heart and make you aware of what's in it. When a change takes place on the inside, it is inevitable that a change must take place

Mental Inversion

on the outside.

The Evolution of Mad Science

When we hear the word "mad", we oftentimes associate that word with anger, but in truth, the word "mad" means to be mentally ill or insane.

→ **Galatians 3:1:** O foolish Galatians, who hath bewitched you, that ye should not obey the truth, before whose eyes Jesus Christ hath been evidently set forth, crucified among you?

In the Bible, the word "bewitched" was only used one time. To be bewitched means to be under a dark spell. It means to be under the power of witchcraft. When Apostle Paul wrote Galatians 3:1, he was rebuking the churches in southern Galatia because false teachers had begun to teach Mosaic law in the churches, which meant, they were turning back to the law in which CHRIST redeemed them from.
The word "bewitched" is directly linked to rebellion, for rebellion is witchcraft. To rebel against GOD means to know the truth, but still choose to follow the lie. Many of the Jews in Galatia knew the truth, yet, they still

allowed false teachers to rise up amongst them and teach in their sanctuaries.

> → **1 Samuel 15:23:** For rebellion is as the sin of witchcraft, and stubbornness is as iniquity and idolatry. Because thou hast rejected the word of the LORD, he hath also rejected thee from being king.

Why is rebellion referred to as witchcraft? After all, traditional media today teaches us that witches are women with pointed noses, bad skin, decaying teeth, and a vendetta against mankind. We've learned to associate witches with the images often depicted on television; therefore, we've learned to associate witchcraft with the women who've been portrayed by the media as witches. But in truth, to rebel against GOD means to utilize the power in which HE gave you against HIM. You have will; you have earthly strength, and your words have power. For this reason, all power that is not in submission to GOD is witchcraft, only some witchcraft is more obvious than other forms of witchcraft. For example, as believers, we know all psychics, sorcerers, palm readers, tarot card readers, and diviners are witches, be they male or female. That's how we have learned to identify witches, but some witches are religious characters who wear priestly garments and quote scriptures. The Bible refers to them as false prophets, false teachers, false apostles, and the like.

To be bewitched means to be perverted, and to be perverted means to operate opposite of the way in which GOD created one to operate. A person who is bewitched either does not know the truth or they are rebelling against the truth, and this makes them mad. Again, the word "mad" means insane or mentally ill, but in truth, we know that a mad person is simply inhabited by demonic spirits. The Bible tells us a story about a man who was full of demonic spirits. By all accounts, the common people labeled him as mad, and they attempted to bind him with chains. Read the story below to learn what happened to that man when he met JESUS.

> → **Mark 5:1-13:** And they came over unto the other side of the sea, into the country of the Gadarenes. And when he was come out of the ship, immediately there met him out of the tombs a man with an unclean spirit, Who had

The Evolution of Mad Science

his dwelling among the tombs; and no man could bind him, no, not with chains: Because that he had been often bound with fetters and chains, and the chains had been plucked asunder by him, and the fetters broken in pieces: neither could any man tame him. And always, night and day, he was in the mountains, and in the tombs, crying, and cutting himself with stones. But when he saw Jesus afar off, he ran and worshipped him, And cried with a loud voice, and said, What have I to do with thee, Jesus, thou Son of the most high God? I adjure thee by God, that thou torment me not. For he said unto him, Come out of the man, thou unclean spirit. And he asked him, What is thy name? And he answered, saying, My name is Legion: for we are many. And he besought him much that he would not send them away out of the country. Now there was there nigh unto the mountains a great herd of swine feeding. And all the devils besought him, saying, Send us into the swine, that we may enter into them. And forthwith Jesus gave them leave. And the unclean spirits went out, and entered into the swine: and the herd ran violently down a steep place into the sea, (they were about two thousand;) and were choked in the sea.

As we can see from the story above, the man was clearly what today's society would write off as mad. What would happen to that man today if he were walking the earth? The answer is evident, because we see people all the time that society has labeled as crazy. Many of them sit idly on the sidewalks mumbling to themselves as we pass them by. Many of them are locked away in mental asylums, while others are in prison. They are bewitched souls who are possessed by demonic spirits, nothing more; nothing less. They are obviously bewitched, but there are some characters who aren't so obvious because they have what society labels as a sound mind; nevertheless, they openly and remorselessly rebel against the LORD. Many have grown up knowing the truth, but have turned away from the truth to follow man's doctrine, while others attempt to merge man's doctrine with the gospel. As we live through each trial life throws our way, our character begins to emerge, and this character manifests to display the contents of our hearts. Who we've become isn't necessarily who

The Evolution of Mad Science

we are; who we've become is the direct result of our thinking and how we handle life and all it brings with it. If we remain faithful to GOD through it all, our character emerges to declare us men and women of faith, overcomers, and more than conquerors through CHRIST JESUS. If we allow the hurts, betrayals and losses to define us, our character will emerge to declare us unfaithful victims of wrongful thinking.

Our character is who we've become, and who we've become is identified through our characteristics. Our characteristics are simply the symptoms of our ways of thinking. Consider how disease is oftentimes identified. Not all diseases are diagnosed under microscopes; many diseases are identified by their symptoms. For example, if you walk into a doctor's office with flu-like symptoms, the doctor will ask you a series of questions, check your temperature and consider the seasons. If it happens to be flu season and you are displaying flu-like symptoms, the doctor will likely diagnose you as having the flu. After the diagnosis, the doctor will attempt to restore your body by giving you a prescription for medicines designed to fight or treat the flu. Human beings are the same way. It's easy to identify what's on the inside of a person

The Evolution of Mad Science

based on their words and choices. Every word that escapes our mouths are symptoms of what we have in our hearts. Remember, the WORD says that out of the abundance of the heart, the mouth speaks. The LORD has written us a prescription for wrongful thinking, and that prescription is HIS WORD.

We are all cups, and we're full of something. Whatever we are full of will flow from our lips and our lives. When what's flowing from our lips is not flowing from our lives, our actions rise up and declare us as liars or hypocrites. We are all identifiable creatures, but only those who are familiar with us or our character types will be able to identify us. Of course, our character types are influenced by whatever's in or leading us.

Scientists have tried to identify character types based on lengthy studies performed on everyday people, killers, psychopaths and so on. This is the world's attempt to foresee the behaviors of people, and to diagnose personalities they believe to be a threat to modern society. Of course, most of the world's research is skewed by the world's perception of what is normal versus abnormal behavior. Traits that are deemed abnormal are often labeled as diseases or mental conditions, thus giving scientists the green lights they need to produce treatments. If you'll notice, scientists rarely develop or claim their drugs can cure victims with mental abnormalities; instead, they find treatments. Treatments are drugs that have to be taken for a lifetime to lessen the effects of a condition anytime it flares up. Labeling something as incurable means more money to the scientists who "diagnose" these conditions, more money to the scientists who research and allegedly find treatments for the conditions, more money to the FDA who has to approve or disapprove of the medications, more money to the government as scientists patent their drugs, and more money for the drug makers who mass produce these drugs. Make no mistake about it: This sudden surge of new mental illnesses and abnormalities are more about money than they are about helping people.

One condition that has taken the world by surprise is Attention Deficit Hyperactivity Disorder, better known as ADHD. A British doctor named Dr. Still first recognized ADHD as a disorder in 1902. Over the years, ADHD has been given many names, finally

The Evolution of Mad Science

settling as Attention Deficit Hyperactivity Disorder in 1987. Over the years, treatments such as Ritalin and Adderall have been the number one prescribed medications by doctors for ADHD.

The symptoms of ADHD include:
- Inattentiveness
- Hyperactivity
- Impulsiveness

Of course, any one of those symptoms describes just about every American child today. The truth is, science labels what it does not understand, and it treats any person who stands out from the crowd. In other words, if you or your children don't fit in, the world says something is wrong with you.

When I was married the first time, I was helping my then husband to raise his son who we'll call Larry. Larry was (and is) an intelligent boy who was extremely energetic and impulsive, and he would have been inattentive if he were allowed to be. He fit the mold for ADHD. As a matter of fact, one of Larry's teachers was sure that he had ADHD because he had more energy and jokes than her other students. Larry was comical, and he was more of a risk taker than other children his age. Needless to say, we pulled

The Evolution of Mad Science

Larry from her classroom, because that teacher was so quick to write off a child she didn't understand. While in her classroom, Larry didn't do well because he was the type of child that had to have consequences to consider, and those consequences had to outweigh his impulsive desires to get a few laughs. Additionally, Larry required consistent discipline because, again, he was a risk taker. Now, when Larry knew he'd be consistently disciplined, he behaved himself consistently. Of course, like most children, he'd test adults from time-to-time to see if we'd lightened up a little.

When Larry went to another school and had a more patient and understanding teacher, he ended up on the honor roll. That's because that particular teacher called us every time Larry misbehaved; and needless to say, once Larry realized that his teacher would cut him no slack, he became one of her star students. His teacher would often tell me that if Larry started playing or talking a lot (his two major crimes), she'd tell him that she was going to call me. Larry would then straighten up and do his work.

One of my friends even suggested that Larry had

The Evolution of Mad Science

ADHD after watching him spin around repeatedly, jump up and down while pretending to be a frog, and noticing how much trouble he got into initially. He wasn't like her son who was the same age. But Larry's father and I were firm in our beliefs that Larry was nothing more than a little boy who was extremely intelligent; a child whose mind was a highway of activities. We knew that as he got older, he'd learn to better manage his thoughts. In the meantime, we knew what type of personality he had, so we knew how to parent him. Consistent love and discipline kept Larry happy, but Larry had to have firm adults around him; otherwise, he'd test his limits. He was a good and intelligent child; that's all.

The issue here was clear. One teacher saw a child who was unlike her other students, and having to deal with such a child meant that she'd have to come outside of her understanding. My friend saw a child who wasn't like her child, and she didn't understand why the boys were so different. Another teacher saw an intelligent little boy who simply needed consistent discipline; meaning, he'd be more of a challenge than her other students, and she was up for the challenge. That teacher loved Larry, and she often talked about

The Evolution of Mad Science

how intelligent he was. As a matter of fact, Larry behaved in that teacher's classroom and rarely gave her any problems; whereas, his previous teacher would often be found with her head in her hand.

The world, and many of the people in it, will write off any personalities they do not understand because it's too much work for them to get the understanding they'll need to deal with those personalities. For this reason, it's safe to say that many of the alleged mental illnesses out there today aren't really illnesses; they are simply man's way of saying they don't understand someone.

As a child, I would have been a star candidate for ADHD. The issue was: I was an intelligent child, and my mind was a highway. I couldn't stay focused for too long, but I always stayed focused long enough to get what I needed done before redirecting my attention elsewhere. I was hyperactive, practically fearless, definitely impulsive, and cautiously inattentive. I knew whom I could be inattentive with, and I knew whom I could ignore. I didn't know it then, but I studied my environment and the people in it. I wasn't like other girls; I could be found chasing other

The Evolution of Mad Science

girls during recess with grasshoppers that I'd caught while on the playground. I picked up frogs, caught crickets, unearthed earthworms, killed spiders with my hands, climbed trees, invented toys to play with, and much more. Does this mean that something was wrong with me because I wasn't in the house playing with my Barbie doll? Of course not. I was just different. Thankfully, my mother never took me down to a doctor's office to have me evaluated, because I'm more than sure that if she had taken me, I would have been diagnosed with ADHD.

Sure, there are many doctors who would argue that ADHD and many of the mental ailments being sold to the world today are real conditions, but most of these doctors only have the findings that they were taught in college. They were given a blueprint for disease, and told that certain behaviors merited certain diagnoses. Additionally, they were handed brain scans and told that the scan on the right was normal and the scan on the left was abnormal. In other words, they were given choices as to what they could diagnose their patients with, but they weren't given flexibility to research further.

The Evolution of Mad Science

I had a male Siberian Husky, and when I'd first gotten him, he challenged everything I thought I knew about dogs. My Husky would tear up my furniture, obliterate my toilet paper, dig holes as deep as three feet in depth in my yard; he'd run away any chance he got, he was stubborn, he was intelligent, and he was outside of my understanding. I loved him, but I needed to understand him because every day meant the loss of a piece of furniture, a clothing item, or some important documents. I went on the Internet and read an article about Siberian Huskies, and I was horrified, yet relieved at what I was reading. I came to understand that my dog's behaviors were consistent with his breed. I thought something was wrong with the dog because I'd never had a dog like him before. All my life, I'd had dogs whose behaviors were similar: They panted, played with me, licked my face, rolled over for their belly rubs, and obeyed me when they heard my voice. My husky, on the other hand, would only obey if I was standing close to him. If he was on the other side of the room, he wouldn't obey me; instead, he'd howl or walk away.

I decided to contact the woman who'd written the article, and I told her about my Husky's behaviors.

The Evolution of Mad Science

She assured me that his behaviors were normal, and that I simply needed to buy a book and familiarize myself with Husky traits. I did, and when I finally got an understanding of his traits, it was easier for me to Husky-proof my house.

What's the point of all this? The point is: Science has learned to group dogs into categories based on their physical traits and personalities. You can now read up on the personality traits of the types of dogs you are interested in so that you can make an informed decision before adopting a dog. Needless to say, this is the direction that science is taking mankind.

Nowadays, billions of dollars are being used to research personality types. After a personality type is characterized, scientists then determine whether they believe that personality type to be mentally ill or not. Please understand that most scientists (if not all) take what man has already established as facts, and they continue to build on those findings in order to establish new findings. In the world of science, challenging another scientist's findings is considered to be career suicide. Only the most daring scientists challenge one another, and only the bravest challenge renowned scientists who've won awards for their findings. So, if what was discovered hundreds of years ago is a lie, then every fact built on that foundation is also a lie.

We're all different, and different doesn't always mean better or worse; it simply means we're not the same. At the same time, we know that demonic spirits have traits that help us to identify the types of spirits they are. The Bible talks about lying spirits, spirits of jealousy, familiar spirits, deaf and dumb spirits, spirits of infirmity, and so on. Of course, you'll know what type of spirit you're dealing with if you learn their behaviors, and with some spirits, you don't need to know their behaviors, all you need is a working set of eyes.

The Power of Imaginations

We've been given a powerful tool called imagination. With our imaginations, we can revisit the past or window shop for our future. Of course, we can't move physically through our imaginations, but we can allow our minds to go into places that our bodies can't go into. One of the reasons GOD gave us the ability to imagine a thing is to help us establish our faith. Man won't believe what he can't see, so our imaginations give us the opportunity to see whatever we want to see in our mind's eye. After we've imagined a thing, it is easier for us to believe GOD for it. For example, if you had a puppy and he got stuck in a drainpipe, you would imagine ways in which you can free him. If you couldn't imagine freeing him, you wouldn't believe that you could free him. If someone had kidnapped you, your imagination would help you to explore ways to escape. If you were working at a dead-end job, making only enough money to pay your month-to-month bills, your imagination would show you the possibilities of a better future. Your imagination is a mall, and what you get out of that mall depends on

The Power of Imaginations

how much faith you have.

Just imagining something isn't enough; you still need faith to believe that what you see in your mind can be manifested in your reality. But the enemy always comes to show you what could go wrong, and he does this to get you to fear him and doubt GOD. The reason the enemy wants you to fear him is because fear is a form of reverence. We all know that Satan is jealous of GOD; therefore, anything we are supposed to give to GOD, the enemy attempts to get it for himself. Fear is faith in the devil. To fear what the enemy says is to exalt his doctrine (lies) above the WORD of GOD (truth).

To get faith, you must have the WORD of GOD; otherwise, your imagination will go into some dark places and bring back some dark things into your life. For this reason, GOD told us to cast down imaginations that come against HIS WORD. *"Casting down imaginations, and every high thing that exalteth itself against the knowledge of God, and bringing into captivity every thought to the obedience of Christ; and having in a readiness to revenge all disobedience, when your obedience is fulfilled" (2 Corinthians 10:5-6).*

The Power of Imaginations

Any imagination that's not cast down will eventually find its way into the heart, and once it's in the heart, it will have to be cast out. This means that it becomes a heart condition that can't simply be rebuked; the person with this condition would have to be delivered. This is to demonstrate to us just how powerful our imaginations are.

Anytime we imagine something, we either desire what we've imagined or we don't want what we've imagined to manifest in our lives. Once we've imagined something, we will trust GOD to bring or not to bring that thing to pass in our lives, or we'll perform the works to bring or not to bring what we've imagined into our lives. Of course, to trust GOD means to be still and know that HE (YAHWEH) is GOD. To trust in one's self is to not trust GOD and be moved by fear. For this reason, the Bible tells us not to lean to our own understandings. When we lean to our own understandings, we begin to imagine strategies and make plans to fix whatever we feel that needs fixing, thus, not allowing GOD the opportunity to get the glory in that situation.

→ **Proverbs 10:24:** The fear of the wicked, it shall

The Power of Imaginations

come upon him: but the desire of the righteous shall be granted.

As believers, we shouldn't fear anything or anyone but GOD, for the fear of GOD is reverence to GOD; it is acknowledging who HE is. The fear of GOD is the only fear that's deemed holy. The Bible tells us that the desire of the righteous will be granted for him. This means that (1) we should always walk in faith, for it is our faith in JESUS CHRIST that renders us righteous, and (2) we should always allow ourselves to have desires. Of course, we must make sure our desires match up with the will of GOD. We can't covet something or someone and expect GOD to grant us the desires of our wicked hearts; GOD only grants the desires of a righteous heart.

What should we do then? That's simple: Never be afraid to dream, and never be so entangled in man's perception of who you are and how far you should go that you stop dreaming big. The average believer only believes to achieve only that in which their parents have achieved, or maybe a little more. That's because we are often surrounded by people who have their perceptions of us, and anytime we attempt to go

The Power of Imaginations

outside of their limited imaginations, we offend them. Now, if you talk with the average person, they will gladly state that they aren't moved by the perception of their friends and family, but in truth, they are. Most people take their ideas, visions, and even prophetic messages to the people they love, trust, or want to impress. In doing so, they give people the green light to express their opinions or redirect them entirely.

Some years ago, I'd just begun seeing a profit from my graphic design services. I was happy about all that GOD was doing in and through me, and just like most women, I wanted to share my joy with my friends. Anytime GOD would give me another book to write, business to start, or idea to implement, I'd call the people closest to me because I was bubbling over with excitement. I couldn't wait to be all that GOD had created me to be. I remember calling one friend about a book GOD had laid it upon my heart to write, and I could hear the disapproval in her voice. After I finished announcing GOD'S plans for me, there was silence on the line. I knew this was her way of showing her distaste for the idea of me being an author. I broke the silence, asking my friend if she were still on the line, and she replied "Yes. That's

The Power of Imaginations

good." Even though she offered approving words, I could tell that she was not in the least bit happy for me.

After hanging up the line, I found myself feeling more and more discouraged. I didn't realize what had happened; I only knew that I was supposed to write a book, but I didn't know when. Because the life was sucked out of my joy, I put off writing that book. Of course, at that time, I wasn't spiritually mature, so I kept the plans to write the book in my heart; all the while, moving on to other things.

A year or more later, the LORD laid it upon my heart again to write that book, so I called another friend. This friend was male, and I knew that he'd always been as honest as he could be with me, and he wasn't burdened by jealousy or any other hindering emotions. He listened quietly as I joyfully recanted what the LORD told me. When I was finished talking, he said something to the likes of, "Sis, I know you're excited and I'm excited for you, but be careful who you tell GOD'S plans for you to. Some people won't be happy for you, and when you hang up the line, they'll be speaking word curses against what you told them. All of a sudden, you'll find yourself losing interest in what GOD told you to do. Sometimes, by telling folks stuff, you may not realize that you are talking to the devil himself, and you'll be showing him how, when, and where to attack you." I was amazed. My mind immediately fell on that friend who I'd previously told about my plans. Surely, the energy and excitement I had before I'd called her was gone after I'd hung up the line. Surely, she never asked me what happened to me writing the book. Surely, I'd handed GOD'S plans for me over to the enemy when I'd relinquished that information to her. I thanked my friend for the words or encouragement, and to this day, I am not forthcoming with what GOD has instructed me to do.

Years later, I would tell another friend about a new opportunity that GOD had opened up for me. I was overjoyed and thought she'd be happy for me. After all, the two of us wanted many of the same things. I'd just received a camera and was about to get into photography. I felt that I could tell her about my new blessing because it had already manifested in the form of a camera. In telling her, I got a chance to see her feelings towards everything I was doing. I don't remember who called whom, but I do remember being extremely overjoyed as I told her about my new camera and the fact that I was about to be a photographer. The line was silent for a few seconds, and then, she spoke. "I don't mean any harm, but don't you think you're trying to do too much?!" I was shocked. I'd always been that supportive friend that my friends could call anytime, and whenever they were blessed, I celebrated louder than them. I didn't understand the idea of discouraging someone to be as blessed as GOD called them to be.

Dream-Killers

That's when I learned that GOD favored me because I celebrated the success of those around me. Needless to say, I began to separate myself from those friends who'd attempted to kill my dreams. They were friends with who I was (the old me), but they wanted no part of the woman that I was becoming.

By that time, I'd matured a lot, and I didn't let her words discourage me in the slightest. If anything, her words were confirmation to me that I needed to end that friendship if I wanted to do everything that GOD had laid upon my heart to do. You see, I still had other dreams, dreams in which I hadn't shared with my

The Power of Imaginations

friends. I'd taken my male friend's advice; often playing it in my mind over and over again anytime some new blessing was on the horizon. There were many days that I wanted to yell to anyone who had ears about what GOD was doing in my life, but I had to learn to be silent.

To this day, anytime I deal with people, I make a special effort to celebrate them when they share their good news with me. For that reason, many people call me to share their good news before they call anyone else. They know that I will be genuinely happy for them.

Please understand that many of the people around you are dream-killers; that is, unless the LORD has delivered you. The enemy loves to surround the wheat with tares in the hopes that the wheat will mingle with the tares and lose its flavor. You will never know who's truly your friend until you've been elevated and demoted. Some people will be there for you when you are hurting or if you've been demoted because their joy is in your pain. They may not show it, but once they are out of your presence or off the phone line, they won't be able to contain their joy. I've had people in my life that I've gone to when I was

The Power of Imaginations

hurting, only to notice that their spirits seemed to be lifted in my pain. As a matter of fact, whenever I was in pain, I noticed the same group of people calling me to check in on me, but they were rarely around whenever I was promoted. They seemed to be allergic to my happiness, or anyone's happiness, for that matter. I went to the LORD about this, and HE explained it this way: Some people live in misery, so when you're miserable, you are in their zip codes. It is then that they can relate to you the most; therefore, whenever joy starts to lift you up, they will attempt to bring you back down by encouraging you to question or reject any opportunities to escape your misery. Those people were not my friends; they are well-disguised enemies masquerading as friends.

I'm strong-willed, and this has posed as a problem for many people who've attempted to redirect my thoughts, messages, or the like. But amazingly enough, I'd been swayed many times by the opinions (expressed or unexpressed) of my friends, family, and colleagues. Of course, this happened when I wasn't mature, but at the same time, I didn't recognize what was happening back then. I only noticed that I would get excited about doing something and suddenly, that

The Power of Imaginations

joy would fizzle out. I battled with procrastination and I blamed that on generational thinking, but once I asked GOD to remove procrastination out of my life, it was then that HE matured me and I stopped volunteering information to people. Nowadays, no one knows my plans but GOD. I only tell people what I'm doing after it's done. Even though the enemy can't stop me (or you) from doing whatever GOD said we'd do, he can (and will) send attacks, distractions, and discouragements to get you to delay obeying GOD. Delaying to do what GOD told you to do is just as bad as not doing it at all.

The point is: You should NEVER tell anyone what GOD has told you UNLESS HE tells you to release that information. Some of the greatest ideas you've had in your life is buried under some man or woman's perception. Please understand that the people closest to you will sometimes not want to see you be promoted because they're worried that they may lose your friendship. All the same, some people are just plain jealous and proud of it.

Your imagination shows you many opportunities that GOD wants to give you, but you can't have anything

The Power of Imaginations

that you refuse to believe GOD for. Additionally, doing the same things with the same people only ensures you'll get the same results that you've been getting. Sometimes, you need to venture outside of your understanding and everything that's familiar to you so you can familiarize yourself with a new understanding, new people, and new possibilities. You can't dream about what you don't know. If you want a mansion, pray about it, believe GOD for it, and continue expanding your knowledge. If you want a bigger ministry, pray about it, believe GOD for it, and continue to let the WORD into your heart. Please understand that as the WORD comes in, there will be times when you are not comfortable with whatever GOD is sharing with and through you because you'll know that the message won't be easily received by people. But you're not in the pulpit or in the streets to serve messages to itching ears; you are out and about your FATHER'S business. Whatever you ask GOD for, ask HIM to give it to you in accordance with HIS will; meaning, HE will position you to not only receive what you're praying for, but HE will also position you in HIS will to do whatever HE'S called you to do. Many times, we don't see what we want because we're not in position to get what we need.

The Power of Imaginations

→ **Mark 11:24:** Therefore I say unto you, What things soever ye desire, when ye pray, believe that ye receive them, and ye shall have them.

Whatever desires you have, you need to ask GOD for them to manifest, and then, you need to believe GOD for them. Whatever you don't have, it's likely because you didn't ask for it, or you asked for it for the wrong reason. *"Ye ask, and receive not, because ye ask amiss, that ye may consume it upon your lusts" (James 4:3).*

To ask amiss means to ask inappropriately. In James 4:3, the LORD tells us what is inappropriate, and that is to ask for something to consume it upon our lusts. For example, if you go to GOD asking HIM to bless you with a bigger house, HE is not only going to hear your prayers, but HE'S also going to look at what's behind the wheels of your prayers. If you're asking for that bigger house because one of your friends has a big house and you're jealous, your prayer is amiss, for it is inappropriate. If you ask the LORD to make you skinnier, and HE looks behind the wheel of your heart and sees that you are lusting after some man, your prayer is amiss. If you ask the LORD to bless you with

The Power of Imaginations

a better paying job, and HE looks behind the wheel of your prayer and sees Mammon (the spirit behind the love of money), your prayer is amiss. Always check your heart before you approach the Throne of GOD. Ask yourself why you want whatever you're asking for. Additionally, you shouldn't ask to be blessed if you refuse to be a blessing.

Your imaginations are powerful enough to manifest as your reality. Be careful what you allow to play in your mind. You have the ability to cast out imaginations. Sure, those imaginations will sometimes return and attempt to earn your trust again and again, but every time an ungodly imagination connects with your mind, disconnect it and replace it with the WORD of GOD. Keep warring against the enemy for your mind and don't stop until he's had enough.

The Horror of Horoscopes

To understand horoscopes, we must understand the origin of horoscopes. Horoscopes are believed to have started in Babylonian culture. As a matter of fact, the oldest astrological charts can be traced back to Babylon.

The word "horoscope" was derived from the Greek words "hõra" and "scopos"; meaning, "time" and "observer". Therefore, horoscope means "an observer of time."
Leviticus 19:26 warns us: *"Ye shall not eat any thing with the blood: neither shall ye use enchantment, nor observe times."*
Observing time is witchcraft. A witch tries to study the patterns of GOD so that he or she can duplicate those patterns. A witch looks for common traits in people, events and things based on time charts, calendars, and the like. They also look for commonalities amongst people, times, and events so that they can draw a conclusion and sell it to others. By doing this, a person in witchcraft attempts to decode the way

The Horror of Horoscopes

GOD works. Of course, no one can understand GOD or HIS ways, so they illegally tap into the spirit realm and commune with familiar spirits. They bring back lies seasoned with facts and sell them to hungry, unsuspecting people. The people who open their minds and their hearts to receive horoscopes unknowingly open their homes, finances, and their lives to familiar spirits on assignment. Familiar spirits stay with families for hundreds and sometimes thousands of years; that is, until someone in that family repents and surrenders wholeheartedly to GOD.

Today, many believers religiously read their horoscopes, and even when warned about the spirits associated with horoscopes, they continue to read and believe the reports of witches. They then turn to the Bible and repeat a resounding "amen" as they read scripture behind scripture. They believe that going to church, reading their Bibles, and speaking religious gibberish is enough to convince GOD to overlook HIS own WORD and let them into the pearly gates of Heaven. After all, that's all they want from GOD. They don't care about having an actual relationship with GOD; they simply want to go to

Heaven, and GOD knows this. In other words, they are attempting to deceive the Almighty and All-knowing GOD, and they are attempting to use HIM. But their hearts are in all-things-Satan. They love the world and all that it has to offer. Their thoughts and their ways are dark, yet, they do know and understand that there is a GOD who sits on high, so they attempt to live for Satan while calling on the name of the LORD. What many don't realize is even the devils believe, and they tremble! But does that mean those devils will go to Heaven? Not at all! Hell was arranged for Satan and his angels (devils).

What happens when you read a horoscope?
- **Your heart isn't guarded**; therefore, it's overtaken and ruled by darkness. Everything that flows from your mouth and your life will represent whatever you have allowed in your heart.
Proverbs 4:23: Keep thy heart with all diligence; for out of it are the issues of life.
- **You become a house divided.** Here's the truth: You cannot serve GOD and Satan; you cannot serve two gods! You are a temple, a house that is inhabited by the HOLY SPIRIT.

The Horror of Horoscopes

But when your house is divided, you will become double-minded and unstable in all your ways. Your fall would be inevitable.
Mark 3:25: If a house is divided against itself, that house cannot stand.

- **You become lukewarm.** What does it mean to be lukewarm? It means that you are attempting to be neutral; to serve whatever god you feel that suits you at any given moment. It means to not be sold out for GOD, but to be a confused sellout to the enemy. When you're lukewarm, you lose your place amongst the righteous; therefore, becoming nothing more than an unbeliever who looks and sounds like a believer, but in order to be a believer, you must first believe. Obviously, if you are leaning to the devil for a word, you don't believe GOD. Revelation: 3:16: So then because thou art lukewarm, and neither cold nor hot, I will spue thee out of my mouth.
- **CHRIST disassociates HIMSELF from you.** Now, this is where the religious lines are drawn, and true believers and religious believers are separated. Many people say that once you're saved, you're always saved, but

this is a lie! In Revelation 3:16, CHRIST said that because you are lukewarm, HE will spue (spit) you out of HIS mouth; meaning, HE will not own up to you before the FATHER who art in Heaven. CHRIST is the Way; HE is the only way to the FATHER. Make no mistake about it: HE didn't leave you; you left HIM when you decided to make the devil's doctrine a part of your life.

John 14:6: Jesus saith unto him, I am the way, the truth, and the life: **no** man cometh unto the Father, but by me.

- **Your house becomes overrun by demonic spirits.** Face it: You can't invite the devil in and then kick him out on Sundays. Devils are spiritual beings, and as such, they are illegal in the earth realm. For this reason, we (believers) can take authority over any unclean spirit, bind it, and cast it into the pit until Judgment Day. Whatever we bind on earth is bound in Heaven, and whatever we loose on earth is loosed in Heaven. We can't open the lines of communication with the enemy and expect to disconnect those lines when we want to disconnect. Devils are always looking for

The Horror of Horoscopes

bodies to possess, lives to oppress, and minds to depress. Sin is their permission slip to attack or possess a land. To a devil, the mind of a human being is territory. Through one mind, he is able to seduce, attack, attach himself to, or possess other minds. He does this through that person's familiar associations, for demonic spirits are like infectious diseases; they will spread to anyone who's exposed to them and has not been immunized. As believers, we are immunized from possession, but devils can still attack, seduce, or oppress us. For this reason, anyone who reads horoscopes or participates in any form of astrology not only opens themselves up for the demonic, but they also expose their family to the demonic. Many children go under attack because of what their parents are exposing them to.

Matthew 10:25: It is enough for the disciple that he be as his master, and the servant as his lord. If they have called the master of the house Beelzebub, how much more shall they call them of his household?

- **You become blind to the truth.** You become so encapsulated by darkness that you can no longer see what's causing all of the chaos in your life. Once a person has gone into the darkness of sin, they begin to get used to walking in darkness. Because they can't see what's causing them to be hindered, they begin blaming others for their downfalls, even blaming GOD. Their finances, health, and sanity all begin to fail, but yet, they still won't repent because, in their minds, they are Christians. They don't see the error of their ways, so they keep going to church religiously and using religious speech, but their hearts are far from GOD.

Proverbs 4:19: The way of the wicked is as darkness: they know not at what they stumble.

- **You may end up with a reprobate mind to match your unrepentant heart.** If you refuse to repent, GOD may wash HIS hands of you (spue you out of HIS mouth) and leave you to a reprobate mind. What does the word "reprobate" mean? Merriam Webster Dictionary defines reprobate as: (1) to condemn strongly as unworthy, unacceptable, or evil (2) to foreordain to damnation (3) to refuse to accept. Have you ever met someone that no matter

The Horror of Horoscopes

what happens to them, they refuse to repent? Along with others, you've watched this person survive situations others wouldn't have survived, and you wonder how and why they could even consider remaining in their sinful state of minds. They curse and speak scriptures all in one sentence. They may have been given over to a reprobate mind because they were given chance after chance to repent, but they refused. To have a reprobate mind means that GOD is no longer drawing them to HIM. HE let sin have them, because they refused to let go of their sin.

Romans 1:28-32: And even as they did not like to retain God in their knowledge, God gave them over to a reprobate mind, to do those things which are not convenient; being filled with all unrighteousness, fornication, wickedness, covetousness, maliciousness; full of envy, murder, debate, deceit, malignity; whisperers, backbiters, haters of God, despiteful, proud, boasters, inventors of evil things, disobedient to parents, without understanding, covenant breakers, without natural affection, implacable, unmerciful: Who knowing the judgment of God, that they which commit such things are worthy of death, not only do the same, but have pleasure in them that do them.

- **You end up depending on witches because of your reprobate mind.** Saul ended up with a reprobate mind, for the Bible tells us that GOD left Saul. He then turned to the Witch of Endor in an attempt to hear from GOD through Samuel. You'd be amazed at the amount of Godless people who've turned to witchcraft in an attempt to hear from GOD. Many of them run churches today. In their attempts to reconnect with GOD, they have launched ministries where they knowingly or unknowingly impart the darkness on their lives to unsuspecting believers. They memorize scriptures and study the ways of other preachers and teachers because they want to look and sound holy enough to sway the people of GOD in their favor. They believe that by teaching GOD'S people, they will have earned favor and forgiveness from GOD. Some of them do this in an attempt to ransom GOD or get revenge against GOD. The people in submission to their ministries suffer one attack behind the other because they didn't pray about that ministry before joining it or participating in it. Leaders with reprobate minds are oftentimes very driven, and will seek to ascend the ranks of the church; oftentimes, going from one church to the other. They want to be Apostles, and they'll seek to get this title by quitting one church and joining another, finally, going online to attain their apostolic ordination. If you've ever come across such a character, you'll notice that they are often very paranoid. They believe that others are after them, the government has a hit out on them, or their family members are plotting against them. In many cases, they separate themselves from the church and attempt to start their own churches.

- **Peace escapes you.** Peace is still, and when you are going from one doctrine to another, you leave peace behind in your pursuit of your own version of the truth. One of the worst things to lose is your peace. Peace is a blessing given to us by GOD, but when there's no GOD, there's no peace. The opposite of peace is fear, just as fear is the opposite of faith. Peace and faith go hand and hand because one cannot have peace without first having faith. So, a person who has lost their peace is a person who has lost their faith. Such a soul will live in the fear of uncertainty.

2 Timothy 1:7: For God hath not given us the spirit of fear; but of power, and of love, and of a sound mind.

- **Death starts making its rounds in your household.** Believe it or not, whatever you are, you will teach others to be. So, if you're a mother and you're reading horoscopes, you are in the same teaching your children to depend on the powers of darkness. Satan did not come to the earth to give life; he came to kill, steal, and destroy. Please understand that devils put price tags on their doctrines, so when you're tapping into horoscopes, you are in the same agreeing to pay those familiar spirits whatever they are asking for. The price that a devil places on witchcraft is one you can't afford to pay. What do they want? Possession of your soul, of course. The enemy wants to steal everything from you that the LORD has given

The Horror of Horoscopes

you. The enemy wants to kill you, and the enemy wants to destroy your soul in hell. To destroy the soul doesn't mean that it ceases to exist; to destroy the soul means to eternally condemn it to hell where there is no hope or remedy.
Romans 6:23: For the wages of sin is death; but the gift of God is eternal life through Jesus Christ our Lord.

Believe it or not, horoscopes aren't just some harmless tools you can use to peek into your future; horoscopes are observers of time (devils) that one uses to determine their future. Whatever a devil proclaims for you via a horoscope is what that devil wants to bring upon you. Sure, you may get a few pleasant messages, but those messages are designed to lure you in. Once you're lured in, the enemy will then begin to unleash his hatred of you against your family and yourself. By then, it's too late to start rebuking him; after all, you can't rebuke the devil if you're sleeping with him. It is so very common to see people reading their horoscopes or hear them talking about their astrological signs, only to find them under attack and rebuking the devil. That's like having an argument with your boyfriend. As soon as things cool off, you'll be in his arms and recanting everything you've said to him. People who read horoscopes and go to church are people who simply have an unstable relationship with the devil. They keep threatening the enemy that if he doesn't straighten up, they're going to give their lives to the LORD. Their church attendance is nothing more than them threatening to make good on their threats. Again, we cannot serve two gods.

> **Joshua 24:15:** And if it seem evil unto you to serve the LORD, choose you this day whom ye will serve; whether the gods which your fathers served that *were* on the other side of the flood, or the gods of the Amorites, in whose land ye dwell: but as for me and my house, we will serve the LORD.

Mental Occupation

According to Google, the word "occupy" means to fill or preoccupy. Other synonyms include: engage, busy, employ, distract, absorb, engross, preoccupy, hold, interest, involve, entertain, amuse, divert.

Please understand that the enemy is after your mind, for the mind is the engine of a man. The mind is where our decisions take place; it is the waiting room for our imaginations and the starting point of our beliefs. Sure, the heart (the control center of the mind) is the enemy's ultimate goal, but if he can inhabit the mind of a man, he can choose and change whatever is allowed into that man's heart.

The music wouldn't stop playing in my head. I'd stopped listening to secular music years prior to this event, but every time I heard a song I once loved, it would occupy my mind, and I'd spend hours, sometimes days, trying to get it out of my head. I kept rebuking the song, and every time one song went off, another one would start playing. Oh, how I wish I

Mental Occupation

could just eject those lyrics the same way I could eject a CD, but it wasn't that simple. I'd allowed that music in my heart some years ago, and now, it was haunting me.

I began to hum gospel tunes over my thoughts. I rebuked my thoughts and even prayed against the music; nevertheless, it would only stop for a few hours or a few days, only to come back and start playing again. Why couldn't I gain control of my mind? Was there something wrong with me? I'd go to YouTube to play Christian songs just so that I could get a better handle on my thoughts. Scenarios like this are common for believers today.

I gathered my thoughts together as I started singing a gospel tune. This was the first of many fights I'd have to endure as I attempted to drench my mind in holiness.

Every time a car would pass by playing a song I was familiar with, that song would start playing in my mind. Every time I was in a store, and that store started playing a song I was familiar with, that song would start playing in my mind. If I allowed myself to drift, I

Mental Occupation

could tell you a lot about what I was into and who I was into it with during that song's reign in my life. I've turned away from secular music completely, and nowadays, I don't like to hear it at all because I don't want to battle it in my mind.

What happened was I'd allowed certain songs to enter my heart when I was in the world. The heart is like the hard drive of a computer: You can delete the music from your life, but it'll always be stored away on your heart's hard drive. The songs I've allowed into my heart are still in my heart, except they are dormant files stored away in my heart's recycle bin; a bin in which only JESUS can empty. As much as I wish the heart had an eject button, it doesn't; therefore, I know why it is important to guard one's heart.

The mind gets information from two directions: the spirit realm and the soulish realm. When we get information from the spirit realm, we must first question or challenge what spirit we are receiving information from. Is it from GOD or is it from the enemy? *"Beloved, believe not every spirit, but try the spirits whether they are of God..." (1 John 4:1).* When we receive information from the soulish realm,

Mental Occupation

it'll either come from the mouths of people or whatever we have stored up in our hearts. A belief doesn't just visit the mind when it's needed; a belief will influence every decision you make. So before you can do anything about any information you're receiving, you first need to discern or ask GOD about the direction of the information. Is it coming from your heart? If so, that's a heart condition in which you have to be delivered from. Is it coming from Satan or his devils? That's an attempted attack against your mind. You simply overcome the enemy by throwing the Sword of GOD (the WORD) at him, just as JESUS did when Satan tried to tempt HIM. Is it coming from GOD? If so, you need to listen, take notes, and ask GOD for understanding. Finally, you need to obey GOD.

The issue with most people is they don't know which direction the information is coming from that they are being fed. Many false prophets and teachers do not try the spirits that are speaking with them; therefore, they call every voice God. A woman once told a family member of mine that she'd been waiting a decade for a man to leave his wife. According to her, GOD had revealed to her that the man she was waiting for was her husband and he was going to leave his wife one day. She claimed that she'd never had an affair with the man, but she was just obediently and patiently waiting for some woman's husband to become her own. Was that GOD speaking with her? No way! GOD will never go against HIS own WORD. GOD hates divorce. So, whose voice did she hear? The answer is obvious: If you're not hearing from GOD, you are hearing from the enemy. She obviously didn't try the spirit by the spirit, because what that force said to her was something that she already had in her heart. She was lusting after a married man, and the enemy knew this, so he successfully got her to pawn herself away, and wait the termination of another woman's marriage. Of course, I knew to intercede on that man's behalf because he probably didn't know that there was a woman out there praying for the destruction of his marriage because she thought she was hearing from the Almighty GOD. When someone says that GOD told them something, you need to understand that there are many gods in the earth. Which god are they speaking of? We serve the only true and living GOD (JEHOVAH), but when some people say "god", they are not speaking of JEHOVAH; they are speaking of whatever force they've learned to

Mental Occupation

depend on or reverence.

You'll notice that the enemy is always trying to preoccupy your mind with something, and oftentimes that something is minor, even though the enemy will make it a major event in your mind. For example, you may have a friend who hasn't called you for a few days, and all of a sudden, you become preoccupied with thoughts of that friend. Now, you're wondering what you did wrong; you're revisiting conversations you had with that friend in your mind, and you're calling your friend to try to find out if something is wrong. There were some things that you were supposed to do on those days, but they didn't feel as important to you as resolving whatever matter had arisen between you and your friend.

You call your friend, and she doesn't answer the phone. Once again, she sends you to her voice mailbox, where you are forced to listen to a happier-sounding her tell you to leave your name and number after the tone. Days pass, and you still haven't heard from your long-lost friend, so you take to talking with your other friends about her. Why was she suddenly avoiding your calls? Why hasn't she returned any of your calls? Opportunity passes you by, and now,

Mental Occupation

you've disobeyed GOD for the sake of a friendship that's likely expired.

One day, your friend calls you back to apologize to you, and she says to you that she's just been going through a lot and didn't want to talk with anyone. She assures you that she's not angry with you; she's just been avoiding your calls because she really didn't want to talk. What happened in this situation? Satan knew just how much you relied on those daily calls. He knew that if he could pull your friend away from you that you'd become so obsessed with reconciling your friendship that you'd overlook that giant blessing sitting on your lap. It worked. Now, you've kept your friend, but you've lost your blessing.

The purpose of preoccupying someone's mind is to distract them. The enemy usually overwhelms a person whenever he sees something manifesting for them. Like a game of cards, the enemy has players stationed all around believers, and these players are usually those we love and trust the most. As I mentioned earlier, it was during those times when I was being elevated that I was made aware of the people around me. They wanted to keep the old me around, even if that meant pushing me to abort

Mental Occupation

GOD'S plans for myself. Of course, such actions are all done in selfishness. You see, the enemy will tell those close to you that:
- You think you're better than them.
- If you're elevated, you won't have anything to do with them anymore.
- You're trying to steal every opportunity available, and you should be leaving something for them to do.
- You don't deserve to be blessed; especially, more blessed than they are.
- GOD is not blessing you; therefore, it's okay to stand in your way.

There are many distractions sent out by the enemy; for example, if you married a person who was in the world, the enemy will use them as his in-house spy. Anytime a blessing is on the horizon, the enemy will stir up your spouse against you. Who better to talk you out of being blessed than the person you lie down with every night? Your spouse may come in and overwhelm you with every problem underneath the sun. They don't know the enemy is using them. All they know is that a problem has arisen in their minds, and they feel emotionally led to overwhelm you with

Mental Occupation

that problem in their searches for peace of mind. Oftentimes, these will be problems that you can't immediately resolve, and this means that the problem would become an ongoing problem in your marriage. *That's why it's important to wait on GOD for your spouse.*

Another distraction that's commonly tossed against believers is the threat of losing their jobs. You've seen it happen, or maybe it was you that it happened to. A believer works for a company led by unsaved characters. The managers of these companies use their "power" to drive home a message to anyone that's under them: They are in control. But they seem to favor every cursing, fornicating, gossiping, and lying soul in that company. As a matter of fact, having no tact and being explicit seems to be the qualifications for a promotion while under their leadership. The believer works hard, but just like everyone else in that company, the believer makes a few mistakes from time-to-time, but the believers' mistakes are magnified; the unbelievers' mistakes are minimized. It isn't long before the believer realizes that the leader or leaders of that company doesn't favor them, and would love to find any reason to terminate them. So, the believer treads carefully amongst the unsaved, hoping to keep his or her job. They come to work early and leave late, but the inevitable happens: they are terminated, and their overjoyed former managers can hardly contain their glee.

Once the believer gets over the pain and humiliation of having been terminated, they find their peace again. They didn't realize it then, but their minds were so preoccupied with their jobs and the troubles therein that they had began distancing themselves from GOD. They'd spent many days on the phone with their friends talking about the latest occurrences between themselves and their managers. They'd spent many nights repeatedly going over each confrontational event in their minds, trying to find something to help them keep their jobs or maybe expose their managers. The enemy had successfully preoccupied their minds because he knew that they depended on their jobs, but what he didn't know was that GOD allowed him to terminate those believers in HIS attempt to get their minds back on HIM. It is never good for a believer to be subject to an unbeliever.

Mental Occupation

Whatever you place value on, that is the very thing the enemy will attempt or threaten to take away from you at any given moment. His goal is to distract you from something he sees coming your way. His goal is to control you using the things that you love the most. For this reason, GOD doesn't want us to love material things; HE wants us to love HIM and HE wants us to love one another. Whatever we love, we place value on, and when we place value on material things, we give the enemy a handle on us through those things.

One of the ways to change your life, of course, is to change your mind. To change your mind, you need to reassess and reevaluate everything and everyone in your life that you've given value to. Oftentimes, when your peace is challenged, it is challenged by things, situations, and people who've been given too big of a role in your life. Those trials are opportunities to reposition things and relationships. Think about a company. A company is always going to look to make a profit. The greater the profit, the better off the company is. When they have someone in that company who's not bringing in much, or someone who's earning more than they are bringing in, the company will oftentimes attempt to retrain that

Mental Occupation

person. When this doesn't work, the company will likely demote that person. If the company is still not bringing in much of a profit, then the company will layoff or terminate that employee. That's because they are trying to make as great of a profit as they can, and they don't want to break even by having employees who aren't turning much of a profit. It may seem cruel (especially if you're on the firing end), but companies must do this to survive. They aren't in business to give people jobs; they are in business to earn money.

You need to think the same way. Reevaluate each situation, relationship, and friendship and determine whether they add or subtract value from your life. You'll notice that you have friends for every emotion you have: boredom, elation, sadness, and encouragement. Rather than building on your emotional state, you should be tearing down negative emotions in order to establish good habits. For example, boredom friends are idle relationships that don't add value to either party involved. Instead of being bored, find something to do like start a business, learn to cook, travel the world, learn a new language; the possibilities are endless. Friends for

Mental Occupation

sadness are usually people who are miserable themselves, or oftentimes, they are happy people who you use to dump on. Either way, the relationship is unhealthy for the both of you. Remember, CHRIST said that we should bring our troubles to HIM. When you dump on another human being, there isn't much they can do if CHRIST is not involved. Personally, I've had to end a few friendships when I realized that I was that friend who everyone cast their burdens on. This wouldn't have been a problem if they were willing to stay on the line so we could lay each issue at the LORD'S feet, but they didn't want to do that, nor did they want to listen to any counsel I had. They simply needed to pour out their debris somewhere. I remember a couple of times hearing people say that they didn't want to hear anything; they simply needed someone to talk to. They said that in releasing what was on their hearts, they could hear themselves and come up with their own solutions. Of course, I knew that this was unhealthy for me because in such situations, the person who's dumped on ends up carrying all of that negative energy; whereas, the person who was dumping will feel relieved once they disconnect the line. The reason is that GOD created us to need HIM, so whenever we have a problem, we should always bring those problems to HIM. When we take our problems to other believers, the correct response of those believers should be to issue wise counsel and offer to pray with you. The two of you are to come together in the name of the LORD, and that way, HE will be in the midst. HE will carry that problem away, and give you HIS perfect peace. When you allow yourself to become a human landfill, you'll watch your own health decline as you attempt to carry everyone's problems, and when you need help, you won't have anyone to turn to. Why so? Because once someone identifies you in a certain category, they usually won't deal with you when you begin operating outside of whatever role they've assigned to you in their lives.

Anytime you notice that your friends are constantly taking away from you, but are rarely (if ever) giving anything or giving anything of value to you, you should lay that relationship at GOD'S feet and ask HIM what HE wants to do with it. If HE tells you to sacrifice that friendship, do so for the greater good. The goal is to remove and reposition everything and everyone in your life so that GOD can use you at a greater capacity. Don't surround yourself with a bunch of people who are outside of the will of GOD because those people are nothing more than satanic placeholders in your life. When you have peace of mind, you'll have the freedom to reach up your hands of faith and bring down any and everything that GOD is handing you. When the enemy doesn't have many positions in your life through friends, family members, colleagues, or the like, he loses much of his power in your life and you'll become an even greater threat to him and his kingdom. For this reason, people who don't give a greater value to their human relationships than they do to their relationship with GOD are people the enemy fears the most.

Life's Mirages

In my mind, I saw what I wanted, but I didn't know how to get to it. I was lost, unsaved, and broken in every way imaginable. Something amazing kept taking place that I couldn't understand at that time. Who I'd become was constantly being overridden by who GOD had created me to be. I spoke the sinner's language, and I walked the paths of darkness, but my heart was hurting for GOD. It didn't matter how hungry I was for GOD though; in my mind's eye, I'd imagined a wonderful life for myself that would require me to sin first and get saved later... or so I thought. I'd been wrong before. What if my journey was yet another dead-end? What if the man I was lying with ended up being just another crack in my already damaged soul? I could hear the voice of GOD breaking through. HE told me repeatedly that HE loved me. HE told me to stop fornicating, but I didn't know how, and I didn't think to ask HIM. As a matter of fact, I didn't realize that it was HIM that I was hearing. I thought it was the voice of my conscious, so I did what I knew how to do. I ignored the loving voice of GOD to follow the

Life's Mirages

loud and charismatic voice of the enemy. What he was selling seemed better than what GOD was freely handing me. After all, it wasn't free to serve GOD, in my sight. I would have to give up everything I'd sinned to get, including the man I was lying next to. I'd have to end the friendships I'd come to rely on, and I'd have to offend the members of my household because they weren't saved. Giving up the sin seemed almost inconceivable, so I kept sinning and chasing a mirage.

It seemed to work at first. I ended up getting married, and from there, I started trying to win my husband's soul for the LORD. That's because that was the vision that Satan sold me. He told me (like he tells other believers today) that I could sin to get the man, and then, bring him to church with me. Needless to say, that didn't work, and seven years later, we divorced.

Over the course of my first marriage, I'd gotten closer to GOD, and had actually matured somewhat in the WORD, but there still wasn't enough WORD in me to keep me from sinning. After that marriage ended, I tried celibacy, but I had no clue as to how one should be celibate.
I found myself wanting to be married again, but I didn't

Life's Mirages

know anything about soul ties, being positioned to be found, or anything about waiting on GOD for my spouse. So, when I met my second husband, the enemy began to sell me another dream. The mirages continued to spring up in my imagination, and I found myself pursuing each sinful dream with unyielding determination. I was in love... or so I thought. I wanted to get married, and my second husband wanted to get married. He seemed (and promised) to be different from my first husband (and he was), so I bit the hook and let the enemy reel me in. I was overjoyed. I was married again, and this time, I was sure I could win his soul for the LORD. As it would turn out, he was even less interested in GOD than my first husband. He'd come from Catholic roots, and he would always say that once he got back in church, he would follow Catholicism. I spent many days trying to teach him about the roots of Catholicism hoping that he would change his mind. After all, I was still following after the mirage that the enemy had so carefully placed in front of me. It didn't dawn on me that the enemy was selling me the same vision that he'd sold me with my first husband, but only with a different man. Nevertheless, not long after marrying my second husband, GOD began to do a major work in me; a work that would change the way I saw relationships, sin, and GOD HIMSELF.

I began to love the LORD more and more as I pursued the knowledge of HIM each and everyday. I cried out to HIM many nights, constantly attempting to repent for putting men before HIM. HE'D already forgiven me, but I hadn't forgiven myself, so I kept apologizing and promising HIM that if I had to do it all over again, I would never sin against HIM again with my body. It was then that the LORD began to minister to me. HE taught me how to be a wife. HE taught me the truth about marriage and its purpose. HE taught me to love HIM like I'd never loved HIM before. HE changed my heart, and by changing my heart, HE changed my mind. By changing my mind, HE changed the way I saw things and people. My view of my husband changed, and I began to lament for his soul. I realized that I could not save him. The only thing I could do was live the very life I'd been telling him about. As the years passed, I had to lean on GOD more and more in an attempt to save my marriage. Our house had been divided from the start with me wanting to serve GOD and my husband wanting to live life his own way. The mirages slowly began to

Life's Mirages

disappear as my eyes opened to the truth and I saw what was really in front of me. After a while, my prayers began to change. I began to pray to be delivered from the marriage I was in. I asked GOD to deliver me if HE saw that the marriage wasn't going to work. I didn't want an unbelieving man anymore. I wanted GOD... period.

GOD began to speak to me more and more, telling me to apologize to my husband whenever we had disagreements, to be quiet when I wanted to contend, and to tell my husband that I loved him when I wanted to say otherwise. After a while, it became easier and easier, especially after GOD began to deliver me from pride. I thought GOD was positioning me so that HE could save my marriage and save my husband. I didn't know HE was just placing me in HIS will, and from there, HE would give my husband a choice: Come into HIS will to have me or walk away entirely. GOD doesn't divide a marriage, but HE will invite us in HIS will, and when one spouse enters the will of GOD, and the other one doesn't; oftentimes, the marriage doesn't survive. That's why GOD told us that if the unbeliever wants to depart, let them depart. There were many, many days that I wanted to leave,

Life's Mirages

but GOD would tell me to be quiet and be still. Again, HE was positioning me in HIS will, for HE had an amazing plan for me. Needless to say, that marriage ended and my peace was restored entirely.

Over the course of my second marriage, my relationship with GOD had become so strongly rooted that I'd recommitted myself to HIM. After that marriage was finished, I was excited about the idea of doing things GOD'S way. The mirages were gone... finally. They had no power over me anymore because my desires changed. My desires were (and still are) to please the LORD with everything that I am. My desires were to GOD, and I'd locked myself into HIS will, promising that only the man in whom the LORD entrusts to be my spouse will be my spouse. There would be no kissing, no sex, and no behaviors that are unbecoming of a GOD-fearing woman. It was (and is) all about my FATHER who is in Heaven.

What's the point of my testimony? It is to show you just how far outside of the will of GOD that our imaginations can take us. Satan often looks at our lives and listens to our words, and from there, he can easily locate our dry places. Once he recognizes a

Life's Mirages

void or several voids, he'll send one of his own to present himself or herself as a void-filler. It's easy to get ensnared and chase after what you don't have to the point that you lose focus on what you do have. The enemy's goal is to subtract what you have in your life, and add to you the plagues of sorrow: Depression, poverty, sexual perversion, unforgiveness, addiction, low self-esteem, and selfishness. He wants to take your life, your peace of mind, your joy, your health, and your family. He'll distract you with visions of what you want, and in return, you will have to sin against the living GOD. In doing so, he continues to lead you further into the deserts of sin, promising that your drought will be over soon enough. He'll cause you to think that you're getting closer to a breakthrough and that today is not a good day to give up on what you've been working so hard to get. But he has nothing to give you, nothing but more lies and broken promises. He'll match you up with his children, and he'll give you the stuff you want, but it's not free; he wants your soul. At the same time, anything the enemy gives you will come against your peace of mind, but what GOD gives you will give you peace. *"The blessing of the LORD, it maketh rich, and he addeth no sorrow with it"* (Proverbs 10:22).

Life's Mirages

In life, there will be opportunities presented to you, and those opportunities will present themselves as blessings. Sometimes, you'll know that the opportunities aren't from GOD, but the enemy will readily tell you that you can sin, get the blessing, and then repent. The truth is: You can't find a blessing in sin. Everything that looks like a blessing isn't necessarily a blessing. Some things are nothing more than fishing lures dangling in the earth realm. On one end is what you want, and on the other end, stands Satan and his devils hoping that you'll bite. If and when you do bite, the enemy will reel you into his will for you, which of course, is outside of GOD'S will for you. There, he'll make you pay a huge price for whatever he hooked you with. He'll unleash his hatred on you in such a way that you'll come to understand that what you sinned to get just wasn't worth the pain that followed. I've met women who were like the old me; women who thought they could sin their way into a marriage and then repent later. Of course, I warned them, testified to them, and let them choose which direction they wanted to go. The ones who chose sin all ended up pulling away from me because of their humiliation at what they were doing. Months or years later, they'd reach back out to me in agony,

Life's Mirages

apologizing for not listening, and testifying of all the hell they'd been through with the men they'd sinned to get. They didn't understand it at first, but Satan simply found their dry places and showed them mirages. In their minds, they saw themselves sinning with the men of their dreams, marrying those men, and then, leading those men to salvation. They still had sinful desires; therefore, they thought they could introduce their lovers to JESUS CHRIST, and preach against the sins that they were against; all the while, justifying the sins they wanted to partake in. Of course, the sins they were against were the sins that directly affected them such as adultery, reveling, and slothfulness. It wasn't long before the inescapable truth met them face-to-face.

What's leading you? What visions do you have that you are currently following? Are they Godly, or sinful? Believe it or not, at this very moment, you are following something. There's something you're trying to accomplish; some place you believe you will arrive at one day. It's our dreams that keep us following the systems we've created for ourselves each and everyday. Some people dream big, while others only want to make it through the day, but whatever you

Life's Mirages

have driving you will determine where you end up in life. Make sure the WORD of GOD and an unquenchable desire to please the LORD are driving you. Anything else is just a mirage.

Channeling Spirits

The biggest conduit used by the enemy to channel demonic spirits is ignorance. What does the word "ignorance" mean? The root word of "ignorance" is "ignore". Ignorance means to be willfully foolish. In other words, wisdom, knowledge, and understanding is available to a person, but they choose not to indulge in it.

I studied the woman on the music video. Her makeup was flawless and her hair was styled to perfection. I loved everything about her style, and I loved her display of confidence. I was a young woman looking for my identity, and I'd just found another identity to wear. *I'm getting my hair done just like hers*, I thought to myself. I stood to my feet and headed to my bedroom. Just like many nights before, I wanted to practice putting makeup on. I loved to learn new things that I could do with my cosmetics, and I couldn't wait to attempt the style I'd just seen on the woman in the music video.

Channeling Spirits

Perfect! I looked in the mirror and loved what I saw looking back at me. My makeup was flawless, and even though I wasn't going anywhere, I'd just learned a new way to apply eyeshadow.

The weekend finally came, and I couldn't wait to apply my makeup. I went to the beautician and she'd styled my hair to perfection. I wore a long weave and had my bang cut in a v shape. I put on my new (and revealing) outfit, and I felt an awakening of confidence in myself. With stilettos on my feet, I walked out of the door to be the character that I was wearing. I thought I was being myself, only unpredictable. I walked into the club with my friends, and scoped out the place. The club was still somewhat empty because we'd come a little too early. I wasn't too worried, but I was overly determined to have a good time and meet someone who looked just as good as I felt.

As the hours passed, the traffic in the club increased. I noticed a few handsome men walk in, and I silently picked out the one I'd be flirting with that night. He'd be my dance partner and I'd be his Cinderella. I prided myself in showing up at clubs, but not giving my number away. My mind was dark and I was on the prowl. I didn't really go to clubs to meet life partners, but I loved being the center of attention. I didn't know that the men who howled as I walked by weren't really interested in me; they were interested in what was underneath the costume that I was wearing. But believing that they all wanted me sent my confidence through the roof.

And there he was. I spotted a guy leaning up against the wall with his friends. His friends were loud and screaming at almost every half-naked woman that passed them by, but he was the quiet friend. I walked towards the quiet guy as his friends sounded off their mating calls. I reached up and grabbed the collar of my new dance buddy's shirt as his friends howled and patted him on the back. On the dance floor, I was every character I'd learned to be. Lost, broken, and fearful of love, I'd compiled a series of characters I'd met in life or seen on television, and I became each of those characters. I had a personality for every situation. As easy as I looked, I played hard to get. I didn't believe in one-night stands, nor would I even consider the idea of prostituting myself. I wanted to be that fantasy girl that a man could not have; I simply loved being a tease.

Channeling Spirits

What was my problem? I wasn't saved; therefore, I was channeling many personalities that I'd come across in my life. I was channeling spirits through myself, and I did not know it. Was I possessed? No, because I can remember each incident with amazing clarity, but I was demonically led. Of course, once I got saved and began to give my life to the LORD, HE began to deliver me from every spirit and personality that I'd once channeled. It took a while for me to find my way back to myself, and of course, I couldn't find the whole me until I began to find the LORD.

In my darkest hours, many men channeling different celebrities (and their spirits, of course) approached me. Anytime a new rapper or hip-hop artist was at the top of the celebrity pyramid, that artists' personality was channeled through many young men. During my lost days, I met so many people channeling the artists known as Snoop Dogg, Master P, Tupac, and the list goes on. I also met men who channeled R&B artists, just as I met women who channeled many rappers and R&B artists. It was always easy to see who was at the top of the pyramid because that person's personality would be channeled through so many people.

Channeling Spirits

Sin is a pyramid with Satan at the top, and whomever he's using just underneath himself. Everyone who listens to rap, hip-hop, and R&B is affected by the music, and many will begin to channel the behaviors or obey the lyrics of the music. People channel spirits all the time by attempting to channel the personalities, styles, and lifestyles of the celebrities they've learned to idolize. Just as the believer is made in the image of his FATHER, an unbeliever will began to transform into the image of his father, Satan. Every time a new song comes out, a new spirit is channeled through the person singing that song. Every soul that's in submission to that artist will listen to that song and take that spirit into his or her minds, bodies, and lives. Demonic spirits, on the other hand, cannot possess believers, since the HOLY SPIRIT of GOD inhabits us, but believers can be misled, attacked and influenced by demonic spirits. A believer who submits to the dark world will eventually begin to transform into the god they are serving; meaning, they will begin to look, sound, and behave like the world. They will shun holiness and say things like:

- *Only GOD can judge me.*
- *Judge ye not.*
- *Who are you to judge?*

Channeling Spirits

- *GOD knows my heart.*

They will defend the world and anyone who's confident (or foolish) enough to play church while still actively participating in the world. Nevertheless, GOD extends grace to the believer and the unbeliever. Grace is not a license to sin; grace is a period of time extended to us by the LORD to repent, but if we go on sinning and refusing to repent, we'll be judged as lukewarm, and CHRIST said HE would spit us out of HIS mouth.

Nowadays, our youth continues to channel the very characters they've seen on television or heard via their radios. When one celebrity starts a trend, that trend takes off and is picked up by the masses. The demonic spirits behind hip-hop are even being allowed into many churches, as church leadership attempts to reach the youth by channeling spirits they are familiar with. Many ministries try to draw the world by becoming the world, but the LORD told us how to reach the lost.

→ **Jeremiah 31:3:** Long ago, the LORD said to Israel: "I have loved you, my people, with an everlasting love. With unfailing love I have drawn you to myself.

→ **Romans 12:2:** And be not conformed to this world: but be ye transformed by the renewing of your mind, that ye may prove what is that good, and acceptable, and perfect, will of God.

Nowadays, many of the churches are trying to conform to the world in their attempts to draw souls, but are instead being ensnared by their own lustful desires to grow their names and their ministries. I've met many leaders who sound, behave, and look like the world, but when questioned about their behaviors, they justify their ways by saying that one cannot reach a world unless they look like them. This is a lie from the pits of hell! A renewed mind is evidence that CHRIST has cleaned up one's heart, and the words we choose will reflect who's in our hearts. The truth is: Worldly ministers don't lead the world into the church; they lead the church into the world! When I was trying to disassociate myself from the world, having hip-hop artists showing up at church concerts made it that much harder to let it go. Understand that a familiar spirit is just that: familiar. I recognized Satan's music anytime I heard it, whether it was playing on the radio

Channeling Spirits

or at a church concert. When I heard worldly music, my spirit didn't dance; my soul danced because my soul was still being delivered. I didn't want to holy dance to that music; I wanted to dance like I'd once danced in the clubs.

One day, I was ministering to a woman who was struggling with fornication. We talked about the music she was listening to, and she openly professed that some of the gospel and Christian music she'd heard had taken her back to the club in her mind. I could relate to her, and for this reason, I warn others today to be careful what type of gospel music they are listening to. If it makes you reminisce about your party days, then likely, the spirit being channeled through that song is familiar to you, and that's why you recognize it.

I was in Denmark a few years back, and I'd just gotten married to my second husband. We went into a McDonald's to sit down because our train back to Germany would not be leaving for a few hours. While we were in the restaurant, we listened as many American songs played over the intercom, and many of those songs had explicit lyrics. We laughed because it was clear to us that they didn't understand what the artists' were saying, and that's why they'd allowed such profanity to be played in a McDonald's. I understood because English is my first (and only) language (for now). The point is: Many people who've been in the world can recognize worldly music, even when it comes disguised as Christian or gospel music, because it's a language that they understand well. People, who've been in church for a long time, if not all of their lives, won't easily recognize the spirits behind secular music, and that's why it's so easy for them to let that music or its likeness be played in their churches.

Demonic spirits like to attach themselves to the mind because their goal is to control or lead the person they are deceiving. Since demonic spirits don't have earthly bodies, they use people to carry out their assignments. Most of the celebrities (celebrated ones) today are channelers, people who channel the spirits that are in them. If you know who's popular these days, you will know whose spirit each demonically led young man or woman is channeling. Again, when Snoop Dogg was at the top of the pyramid, there were tons of young (and some old) men who spoke like him, behaved like him, and even tried to rap like him. Some of these people even picked up the nickname "Snoop" because they wore his likeness.

I went through years of deliverance from everything I'd once allowed in my heart. There were so many mindsets and personalities in me that I'd lost touch with my own identity. I had to lay each mindset on the altar of GOD, surrendering my whole heart to HIM, and I noticed that the closer I got to GOD, the further I got away from the characters I'd become. Slowly, but surely, I began to remove the layers of costumes I'd been wearing. I began to remove the makeup, weaves, colored contact lenses, and all of the items that made the costume that I wore daily. I began to cover my body up more, until one day, I realized that I didn't like even slightly revealing clothes. What was happening on the inside of me began to manifest itself on the outside. I was changing, and I was beginning to look more like my FATHER (JEHOVAH). To this day, I wear a little makeup from time to time, but nothing like I used to wear and not for the reasons I used to wear it. Nowadays, makeup is nothing more than art to me. I wear hair extensions, but only for braided hairstyles, but not for the reasons I once wore extensions; they are simply upkeep styles that I don't have to worry about styling for months at a time. My contact lenses are medicated, but I don't wear colored contacts anymore. I'm perfectly happy with the color of my own eyes. The point is: A change that occurs on the inside will always be seen on the outside. If you find yourself in the midst of a leader who looks like the world, you'd better believe that the world and every spirit in it is being channeled through him or her.

Gender Channeling & Homosexuality

→ **1 Corinthians 14:33:** For God is not the author of confusion, but of peace, as in all churches of the saints.

In 1 Corinthians 14:33, there are three statements that I want to bring attention to, and they are: *not the author of confusion, GOD is the GOD of peace*, and finally, *as in all churches of the saints.*

GOD is not the author of confusion: We all know what an author is. An author is a person who writes a book, story, article, or the like. In this, we come to understand that GOD is an author, but HE is not the author of confusion. What is HE the Author of then? The WORD of GOD. Every WORD that proceeded from the mouth of GOD is the WORD, otherwise known as: the Doctrine of Truth. To be confused means to be divided between two or more doctrines; it is to be uncertain as to which course you want to take. Anytime we have the opportunity to make a

Gender Channeling & Homosexuality

choice, the enemy has an opportunity to confuse us. When GOD said that HE is not the author of confusion, HE was saying that confusion itself is a doctrine; it is a strategic plan of the enemy to get the people of GOD to doubt GOD. Anytime your mind is not made up in relation to something GOD told you, you are actually considering saying that you think it's possible that GOD may have done the impossible: told a lie. Such thinking is called confusion; meaning, you haven't decided as to whether or not you believe GOD. The enemy doesn't care whether you finally take his side or not, just as long as you're not on GOD'S side because anytime you doubt GOD, you become lukewarm. To be lukewarm is to be outside of the will of GOD, and for this reason, CHRIST said that because you are lukewarm, HE will spit you out of HIS mouth. This indicates that your temperature (mind) has been changing for a while.

With gender roles, many people are confused. We live in a time where it's not uncommon to see effeminate men and masculine women. This is, in no doubt, the work of GOD'S enemy, for the enemy works against the mind of a man (and woman), and he seeks to pervert that mind using confusion.

Gender Channeling & Homosexuality

GOD is the GOD of peace: Confusion is a bridging doctrine between truth and lies. Of course, the spirits directly associated with confusion are spirits of perversion, lying spirits, and anti-Christ spirits. These demonic spirits set out to lead believers or aspiring believers into mental bondage. When a person is on the bridge of confusion, that person does not have a sound mind.

Think of the times when you were torn between two decisions or you hadn't made up your mind about something. One of the things you'll notice is that you were not in a peaceful state anytime a decision had not been made. Once you finalized your decision (be it a right or wrong decision), your mind settled. For example, a man having an adulterous affair may be unstable because he's undecided as to which woman he wants to be with. He won't have peace, and he'll oftentimes attribute his lack of peace to his suspecting wife. Let's say that man finally leaves his wife and moves in with his mistress. He finally makes up his mind that his mistress is the woman he wants to spend his life (or the next few years) with. Finally, the dust settles in his mind, and he's able to go on with his life; that is, of course, until reaping season starts. What happened when he left his wife and made up his mind to be with his mistress? His mind settled, and even though he didn't have complete peace, he had mental security or stability. All the same, a person who finally makes a decision to do what GOD told them to do will find peace once they are no longer considering whatever alternative the enemy has presented to them. That is to say that confusion is a state of insanity; a made up mind is a settled mind because it has taken a position, and a mind found in truth is one that has peace and glorious expectation. Let's revisit the example of the adulterous husband. Because he chose sin, he won't have authentic Godly peace, but he will have a calm: a time in which the war in his mind has ceased and he's able to rest more. Nevertheless, once we make a decision and finalize that decision in our hearts, we have officially taken a position, whether that position be for GOD or against GOD. Because he chose to go against GOD, the WORD of GOD and the Blood of JESUS will be against him; therefore, his calm will end when reaping season starts.

The peace that surpasses all understanding comes with the uncompromisable and unchangeable truth: the WORD of GOD. Once we settle our minds in the

WORD, we can have peace, and we will know that reaping season is a season of good tidings and not almost unbearable consequences.

As in all churches of the saints: The word that sticks out the most in this statement is "all". Of course, we know that the word "all" is an inclusive word that means "every". This means that in every church of GOD, there is peace. Anytime you enter a chaotic church, you will find disorder, confusion, and strife. *"For where envying and strife is, there is confusion and every evil work" (James 3:16).*
Will there occasionally be disorder and confusion in a GOD-ordained church? Most definitely. The enemy will strive to send confusion amongst the members of a congregation and the leadership anytime he sees an opportunity, but the LORD told us in Ephesians 4:26-27 and Matthew 5:23-24 how to get this strife and confusion from amongst us.

- → **Ephesians 4:26-27:** Be ye angry, and sin not: let not the sun go down upon your wrath: Neither give place to the devil.
- → **Matthew 5:23-24:** Therefore if thou bring thy gift to the altar, and there rememberest that thy brother hath ought against thee; leave there

Gender Channeling & Homosexuality

thy gift before the altar, and go thy way; first be reconciled to thy brother, and then come and offer thy gift.

What GOD is telling us is that a Godly institution is one of order. Of course, GOD entrusts the leadership to restore peace and order immediately, never allowing strife to sit amongst the sheep for longer than a day. This means that problem resolution between believers should be instituted immediately and anyone who doesn't love peace should be rebuked.

Our bodies are now the temples of the HOLY SPIRIT; therefore, we are far more valuable to GOD than a church building. For this reason, we have to stay in agreement with the WORD of GOD to remain in peace. This means that we must agree with what GOD said about life and what GOD said about us. If GOD said that you are a woman, the evidence that you are a woman is present on your body. The evidence of your gender is between your legs. If GOD called you a man, the evidence that you are a man is between your legs, for you are whatever GOD has called you. When a person says that they are a man trapped in a woman's body or a woman trapped in a man's body, what that person is saying is they are confused. They see the evidence of what they are between their legs; they've been told that they were one gender all of their lives, but what they see feels like a lie to them. What the enemy is doing to their minds is introducing confusion to them. He's telling them that GOD made a mistake with them; he's claiming that GOD did the one thing the Bible tells us HE cannot do: tell a lie.

Demonic spirits usually start attacking children from the minute they are conceived in their mothers' wombs. When the mother is an unbeliever who struggles with any form of perversion, her child will also battle with perversion. For this reason, you'll notice that many homosexuals were raised in homes where one or both of their parents were sexually perverse. For example, you'll notice that promiscuous women oftentimes bear and raise sexually perverse children. These children grow up battling with promiscuity or homosexuality because perversion was a familiar spirit that lived in their home. That's why so many people say that they were born gay, but the truth is: They were born into homes where perversion ruled. Some people who were brought up in

Gender Channeling & Homosexuality

seemingly GOD-fearing homes grow up being confused about what they are because perversion was allowed in their homes. Perversion is a familiar spirit to them; it is one that they know all-too-well. Their parents simply wore a mask of righteousness, but one or more of their flesh's fruit (children) began to represent the very spirit in which they serve or once served. Now, this isn't to say that every gay or perverse child comes from hypocritical parents; it is to say that the child was subjected to the spirit of perversion for a long time, and in most cases, they picked that spirit up in the comforts (or discomforts) of their own homes. In some cases, the parents were good parents in many ways, but they just weren't discerning enough, so they let people in their homes or lives, and those people ended up molesting or misguiding their children.

When I was younger, I was molested countless times by both boys and girls. I knew that what they were doing to my body was wrong, but at the same time, I began to find pleasure in it. Having grown up in perversion, I understood right from wrong, but I also began to reason with wrong. There were different levels of wrong, in my mind. Because my molesters

Gender Channeling & Homosexuality

were close to my age, oftentimes two or three years older than me, I didn't see it as really wrong; I just saw it as children playing games that mom and dad wouldn't approve of. Wrong, to me, meant being caught doing something and having to suffer the consequences. After a while, I didn't see "bumping clothes," as I referred to it, as wrong; I began to see it as one of the games children played.

As I entered my teen years, my mind began to change. I didn't like being touched anymore; I especially didn't like being touched by girls because my identity was beginning to take shape. I identified myself as a heterosexual woman who wanted to be married, have children, and enjoy the pleasures of sex with my husband. Nevertheless, I was still perverse. Instead of homosexuality, I went into promiscuity. My promiscuity was established through a series of short relationships where I'd been given the "girlfriend" title. I was not into orgies or one night stands. In my mind, those things were far beneath me, but I was still promiscuous because I went from one relationship to the other in search of love.

Other women who'd undergone the molestations and

Gender Channeling & Homosexuality

the experiences I've had went in a different direction, however. They entered sexual relationships with other women, and many of them began to identify themselves as men trapped in women's bodies. The truth is: The same spirit that is on them was once on me, but perversion manifested itself differently in me than it did in them. For me, it manifested as a sexual addiction; whereas, with them, it manifested itself as homosexuality. For this reason, I see homosexuality through GOD'S eyes and not man's perception. Homosexuality is simply a manifestation of sexual perversion and misidentification. It is when the enemy has lied to a person, and they've found comfort in those lies. All the same, it is just as much of a sin as promiscuity or fornication. I could never say that the women who chose homosexuality were more hell-bound than I was when I wasn't saved. We were all hell-bound, only, we were heading towards hell on different routes.

Gender channeling usually starts when a child is young. Many girls refer to themselves as tomboys when they are young, and they'll hang around guys and began to channel the behavior of guys. After a while, they lose who they are as they learn to be something else. Because they aren't boys, they can't really channel boys, so they unknowingly begin to channel demonic spirits called spirits of perversion. Please understand that perversion isn't always sexual. Perversion means to alter the course of something; it is to change the original design and purpose of a thing. If you try to cook spaghetti in a washing machine, you have perverted the purpose of that washing machine. It wasn't created to cook spaghetti. That's how perversion works. It takes a creature that was created for one thing, and recreates in it a new way of thinking that goes against its original, GOD-intended purpose. In other words, it deforms one's thinking, but the WORD of GOD transforms us by renewing our minds.

Once the spirit of perversion finds a home in the mind or heart of a person, it then perverts them in every way, including causing or encouraging them to be sexually perverse. A person who is bound by perversion needs to be delivered from just that: perversion. Once the spirit of perversion has gone out of them, they then have to have their minds renewed because the lifestyles that they were accustomed to living may still look attractive to them; after all, it's

Gender Channeling & Homosexuality

what they know best. As GOD continues to work on their minds, they will find that those lifestyles will began to look more and more unattractive to them, until one day, they discover that they are repulsed by the idea of those lifestyles.

Gender channeling is oftentimes a response or reaction to something going on in a person's mind or something that has gone on in a person's life. Many girls who'd been molested began to act, think, and dress masculine in an attempt to look less attractive to the men who'd been molesting them. This is nothing more than a defense mechanism for them. Some of these girls had to take on the dominant roles in their homes to protect their siblings from the monsters who'd been molesting them. By doing so, they became more and more masculine, and they began to identify themselves as boys. Many young men who'd been molested began to act, think, and dress feminine because their spirits were broken and they'd begun to question their identities. Sometimes, their behaviors were nothing more than an unheard cry for help.

How does one get delivered from perversion and

every spirit associated with perversion? I got delivered from perversion by confessing my sins to GOD, resisting those sexual urges that once were like unquenchable fires to me, and I began to take the WORD of GOD into my heart daily. As my mind changed, my desires changed. When GOD delivered me from perversion, that spirit tried to come back many times, but I continued to reject it, rebuke it, and bind it. One day, I discovered the power of being a child of GOD. I could bind that spirit and cast it into the abyss until the Day of Judgment; meaning, I could stop it from coming after me. I stood in faith and began to come against perversion, and suddenly, those desires didn't try to rise back up again because they'd been destroyed. Nowadays, I am disgusted by what I was, but I am thankful for who I am today. Only GOD could have delivered me from those dark forces that once made it so hard for me to live a normal life. Other men and women I've met who've been delivered from both hetero and homo perversions were delivered in the same way. They came to the knowledge of the truth, and they began to quench their thirst for GOD by partaking in the WORD until perversion could no longer find a welcomed place in their hearts.

Gender Channeling & Homosexuality

They submitted themselves to GOD and resisted the devil and he got up and fled from them (see James 4:7). They surrendered wholeheartedly to GOD, refusing to do those things that are an offense to HIM. In order to know what offends GOD, we must know the WORD of GOD. It's a decision that one makes to give up the very sin that's keeping them estranged from GOD, and that decision may seem difficult at first, but once you start loving GOD more, that decision will be much easier.

If you're a man who sometimes (or all the time) feels womanly, bind and rebuke the spirit of perversion. If you're a woman who sometimes (or all the time) feels manly, bind and rebuke the spirit of perversion. GOD said that whatever we bind on earth is bound in Heaven, and whatever we loose on earth is loosed in Heaven. You have the power within you through CHRIST JESUS to take authority over unclean spirits, bind them, and cast them into the abyss until the day of Judgment. Also, you will need to:
1. **Disassociate yourself from all workers of iniquity.** That's not judging them, that's repositioning yourself to be a light to them.
2. **If you're a woman, be feminine, and if you're**

a man, act masculine. Don't allow yourself to channel those spirits for even one more second. Know this: There are many people out there who've learned to ignore their desires to be with others of the same sex, and these people have leadership roles in churches. They are not delivered! The devils inhabiting or leading them are simply dormant. But their speech and their ways betray the characters they are pretending to be. The men are still feminine, and the women are still masculine. That's because they decided to stop the perverted acts, but they did not bind those perverted spirits that were in or around them. Don't do the same. Be delivered for real.

3. **Get rid of all of the clothes you wore while in your sin, and get a new wardrobe.** I know this sounds outlandish, but anything used as a sacrifice or altar to idols must be destroyed. Believe it or not, those clothes are sacrificial offerings. If you're a man, dress like a man. If you're a woman, dress like a woman.

4. **Always check your thoughts.** Anytime you have those days where you're feeling as if you're manly (women) or you're feeling

Gender Channeling & Homosexuality

womanly (men), go into warfare against perversion. Please understand that demonic spirits do return when allowed. *"When the unclean spirit is gone out of a man, he walketh through dry places, seeking rest, and findeth none. Then he saith, I will return into my house from whence I came out; and when he comes, he findeth it empty, swept, and garnished. Then goeth he, and taketh with himself seven other spirits more wicked than himself, and they enter in and dwell there: and the last state of that man is worse than the first. Even so shall it be also unto this wicked generation"* (Matthew 12:43-46).

5. **Stay focused.** The enemy will use many distractions to try to get you back into his grips. He may even use insensitive believers to say or do things that are an offense to you, and from there, you may find yourself not wanting to be a part of the church. Please understand that not every believer is Godly; some of them are Satanic plants sent out to run confused souls back into the world. If it acts like a devil, it is a devil. Just take whatever lesson GOD gives you from watching them and use that to

minister to others once you've been wholly delivered, of course.

6. **Talk to GOD daily, and tell HIM your thoughts.** You'd be amazed at the power of confession. It is as freeing as the wind, and GOD will use it to blow away every demonic spirit that attempts to find its way into your heart.

→ **Luke 10:19:** Behold, I give unto you power to tread on serpents and scorpions, and over all the power of the enemy: and nothing shall by any means hurt you.

A Changed Reality

Your reality will never change for the better until your mind changes for the better. All too often, we park in mindsets, and we make our homes there, not understanding that our ways of thinking pit us against GOD. Change is uncomfortable, and any change of the mind is one that can sometimes seem unbearable. After all, you've made plans for your life and the lives of the people you love the most, but you've made plans according to your today way of thinking. No matter how grand a plan is to us, that plan is subject to change if it's not GOD'S plan for us. *"There are many devices in a man's heart; nevertheless the counsel of the LORD, that shall stand" (Proverbs 19:21).*

Most of the time when we are being shifted mentally, we go through what appears to be tense realities. For example, we see the ends of friendships that we thought would never end. We send familiar relationships finally being severed, and we feel angry, helpless, and spent. We see romantic relationships

A Changed Reality

being shifted, and if GOD doesn't put them together, we oftentimes watch the ends of those relationships unfold and begin to manifest. We begin to see those threats we'd been receiving on our jobs manifest, and we'll oftentimes see our religious relationships be tried. Everyone who's in our lives religiously instead of purposely is removed. This time can feel a little overwhelming, especially if you don't realize what's going on in your life. It's easy to say the devil is attacking, but in many cases, the enemy is simply being handed back his stuff and his people. All of his plans for us are being destroyed, and ironically enough, we sometimes spend that time crying with him, not understanding that we've just been delivered. Deliverance hurts... *period.* Most people who know they need deliverance refuse to subject themselves to deliverance because they don't want to lose the people, the stuff, and the jobs they've come to love. Nevertheless, when GOD calls us to carry out a task, we have a choice: come out of our comfortable places, be painfully squeezed out of those places, or stay in those places knowing that we are no longer in the will of GOD, which means, we can't enjoy the blessings of GOD from where we are. Being in disobedience is being in a dry place; it is a spiritual

A Changed Reality

desert.

Your reality is simply a manifestation of your way of thinking. If your way of thinking is wrong, the wrong things and people will surround you. It's easy to get comfortable in the wrong mindset amongst the wrong people, but the truth will always drive you back to a crossroad. At that crossroad, you are given the chance, once again, to choose a different path. Most people choose the familiar path, even though they know what awaits them on it, but the few who do choose the unfamiliar path (and don't turn back) go through some hardships, only to arrive in lands flowing with milk and honey. In other words, they find their wealthy places as they venture towards their called places.

Our realities are nothing more than the beds we've created for ourselves to lie in. They are the buildings we've built to dwell in, and if we want to move into a better place, we must first move into a better way of thinking. Of course, we change our minds by changing the information that goes into our minds.

Sometimes, we are forced into new realities; realities

A Changed Reality

we didn't volunteer for. The death of a loved one, the sudden onset of a divorce, or the unforeseen termination of a job are all great examples. In those times, we are being forced to rethink our futures because the people or the jobs we'd planned to have with us are no longer a part of our lives. It is during those times that we are often presented with new opportunities to change our realities by changing our minds. It's easier to step out in a new reality while in pain because we're already in transition. For this reason, GOD is close to us when we are hurting. HE loves us and HE draws closer to us in heartbreak because HE wants us to give HIM the opportunity to put our hearts back together the way HE has designed them to be. *"The LORD is near unto them that are of a broken heart; and saves such as be of a contrite spirit" (Psalms 34:18).*

When GOD tells us to come out of a mindset and accept the truth, we tend to question GOD and we tend to question whether or not we are truly hearing from GOD. In our hearts, we know that we're hearing from HIM, but we'll oftentimes try to delay answering HIM because we hope that by staging a sit-in and refusing to come out that HE'LL let us keep our

A Changed Reality

current lifestyles. If we can only show the LORD just how much our realities and our relationships mean to us, maybe... just maybe, HE'LL let us keep those realities. At least, that's what we tell ourselves, not understanding that we are attempting to throw a tantrum in front of the LORD in the same way a two year old throws a tantrum in front of his or her parents. Needless to say, GOD is not moved (at least on our behalf) by our tantrums, and such behaviors only set us up to be disciplined. It is then that GOD releases something in our lives that we weren't prepared to face: the truth.

When the truth comes, everything we thought we knew is placed under a microscope. Every lie we'd accepted is then brought forward, questioned, and assassinated. We spend so much time trying to revive the lies because accepting the truth means accepting a change in our realities, a change that we aren't emotionally ready for. But when it's time for GOD to push us out of our comfortable nesting places, HE will push us despite our protests. That's why it's better to just get out and start flying the minute the FATHER tells us to test our wings than to stay in a comfortable mindset and be forced out of it. Some new realities

A Changed Reality

can be harsh and unapologetic. Sometimes, being thrown from the nest causes us to endure injuries to our hearts, and even though our wounds will heal in time, we have to endure the pain of those wounds until they heal. Personally, I got tired of being thrown from the nests, so I started spreading my wings the minute the LORD told me to. Sometimes, I believe the FATHER catches me flapping my wings in preparation for flight before HE tells me to fly. That's because I don't want to be outside of HIS will again, and I definitely don't want to be thrown from the nest again because falling feels far worse than landing.

In every new reality, we are blessed with new mindsets, but we can't get too comfortable in those realities because our realities are subject to change at any given time. It is never wise to assume that we're finished being moved or we're finished being shifted. Just like climbing a mountain, we don't just fly to the top and start waving victory flags. Instead, we have to climb up that mountain level by level, and learn to pace our breathing at each new height since air pressure decreases at the top of a mountain. In every new reality we're forced to endure, we are ascending or descending the WORD of GOD, and our level of

A Changed Reality

praise will always match our level of understanding. We must learn to pace our reception of the WORD of GOD in accordance with each new height, or we may find ourselves at new heights unable to breathe in our new realities. In other words, we need to read our Bible more, pray more, and go to the sanctuary more so we'll know how to live in our new realities. Living in the manifestation of a new place without the knowledge of how to live there is what drives so many believers back into their comfortable wildernesses. It's what drives so many believers back outside of the will of GOD and straight into the arms of Satan. From there, they are attacked on every side, and even though they call upon the name of the LORD, they refuse to enter the will of the LORD; therefore, they must face their giants alone. We can't call GOD into sin and ask HIM to fight everything that's coming against us while we're there.

Let go of any mindset the LORD is trying to pull away from you. It may look like the process is going to be unbearable, but it isn't. The hardest part of the process is believing you can't get through it. The easiest part of the process is actually getting through it. When your will matches GOD'S will, the process

A Changed Reality

will be seamless and painless. But when you resist the will of GOD, the process becomes excruciating because the blessings of GOD will not encamp you while you're in sin. Your disobedience is your desert, and you'll have no choice but to either get in the will of GOD or succumb to the elements of your current reality.

As a Man Thinks

My reality didn't match man's understanding or perception of me when I was young. Even though we were poor, I never saw us as poor. I didn't join any gangs or hang out with any cliques while in my old neighborhoods. Sure, I had my friends, but my friends were mostly the people who lived on the same street that I lived on. We all came together to play, we fought each other, we forgave each other, and we lived to play another day. In most of the schools that I went to, I noticed that there was an expectation amongst the people; an expectation for a poor child to act poorly and for a well-to-do child to be praised. When this expectation was not met, a lot of people ended up fighting, persecuting, or ridiculing each other. For example, a child born into a family who *had money*, as we so eloquently put it, was oftentimes expected to be a leader, and the children who had nothing were expected to either follow or be ridiculed by the child whose family *had money*. Of course, no one actually said those words out loud, but it was our reality. For this reason, many children who had nothing either kissed up behind children who seemed to have everything or they fought them. As for me, even though I'd picked up a lot of mindsets from my peers, I never could act as if I had nothing. In my mind, we were rich or we were going to be rich. Because of that mindset, I found myself not being able to fit in with some of my peers. Children who believed they'd never do anything with their lives often befriended other children who didn't believe they'd ever do anything with their lives. They were stuck in a cycle, doomed to repeat their parents' mistakes, so they felt they had absolutely nothing to lose. Such children often hated children who had the same realities as they did, but not the same mindsets. The most common thing said to a child who didn't fit in was, "You think you're better than us." Those words were oftentimes followed up with a few punches, a full-fledged fight, and the establishment of new divisions (cliques). At the same time, well-to-do children wanted nothing to do with children who didn't dress or behave like themselves. I always found myself amongst children who had the potential to do great things, but just like me, they were broken, yet hopeful.

I learned at a young age that I was either very loved

or very hated by my peers because my personality didn't leave much room for tolerance. The issue was I refused to change to fit in. I was just me and I was okay with that. I wasn't into gossip as much as many of my peers were. I fought a lot, but I really wasn't into fighting; meaning, I didn't purposely start fights. I often fought to defend my family, my friends, or myself. At the age of eleven or twelve, I found myself dressing like the professional woman I wanted to be, mixed with the tomboy I'd learned to be. I was extremely girly, but I was always trying to prove a point, so I climbed trees, ran street races, hiked in the neighborhood woods, and pushed myself to do almost anything I wanted to do. I would often be found outside wearing my mother's large earrings, fancy necklaces, a little makeup, a purse, heels, and perfume. At the same time, if I was wearing a skirt, I would wear biker shorts under my skirt so I could climb trees or fight if I had to. It goes without saying that I was a resourceful young woman, a girl who, by industry standards, was a little strange. That's because who I was on the inside bled through who I'd learned to be on the outside, and I didn't try to hide myself from the people who couldn't accept me. Most young children growing up in poor areas where there's a lot of fighting, hide any gifts they have that may draw bullies to them. I didn't hide mine; I just fought with my bullies. I didn't think of myself as a poor child; I didn't think of myself as being less than anyone else, and I didn't try to fit into cliques because I didn't make for a good follower. I had my own mind and my own style, and I only hung around people who could accept me as I was, or at least, pretend to. I was an inventor, oftentimes, creating toys out of whatever we had around the house. I was a seamstress, oftentimes, creating skirts for myself, or little pillows to play with. I was a songwriter, oftentimes, writing songs about my crushes and life experiences. I was a poet, oftentimes, writing poetry about my crushes. I was an artist, oftentimes, drawing a mixture of reality and fantasy. I was a writer, oftentimes, writing little miniature books made of notebook paper and staples. The point is: I was who I was created to be, and I didn't let my present situation dictate who I'd become. I was energetic, and as I mentioned earlier, if I had been taken to a psychiatrist, I likely would have been diagnosed with ADHD because I had so much energy and I had trouble staying focused. There was nothing wrong with me. I was simply created to stand out, and that I did. I had to learn to better manage my thoughts to better process them. For that reason, I often drew the wrong kind of attention from people who "had money" because I wasn't fitting into their perceptions of me. I was a poor girl in a dysfunctional family; a family who moved almost every year because of financial hardships. I wore hand-me-down clothes and I had to style my own hair. For this reason, I often got the attention of and ended up fighting with girls who believed themselves to be superior to myself after they'd approached and ridiculed me. I also ended up fighting with girls who thought I felt superior to them after they'd confronted me about their beliefs. The cycle seemed as endless as it was foolish.

My thoughts of myself slowly became my reality for myself. Sure, there are a lot of things I have yet to see the manifestation of, but I know who I am on the inside, so I know what to expect on the outside. As I thought in my heart, I became, and as I think (presently) in my heart, I am.

The realities many people said I would have ended up became the realities that their children received. Children don't grow up to be who we hope they'd be;

they grow up into whom they really are or what their parents teach them to be. Because most people don't know or understand this, they unintentionally groom their children to be failures. A farmer who understands that he is not planting just another tree in the earth, but is planting a specific kind of tree will know how to better water and position that tree for growth. A farmer who tries to plant one tree where another tree is already planted is a farmer who will soon watch those two trees intertwine into something hideous, or they will see one tree uproot the other. Of course, the trees are the children, and the farmers are the parents. A child's true identity is already locked up inside of them, but it takes a wise person to unlock it.

Whatever you believe you are, you are. That's why Satan fights so fiercely and works so hard to ensure that you believe you are nothing more than what you see in the mirror. He's always fighting your perception of yourself because he knows that whatever you believe about yourself will eventually become your reality. He's always sending friendly enemies into your life to help shape your perception of yourself and GOD because if he can change your mind, he can uproot you and replant you in his will. His will for you is that you pervert as many people as you can, live a miserable life, die, and go to hell. He does understand, however, that it takes layer upon layer of lies and hurt feelings to bring you as low as he wants to bring you, but he's patient. Be very careful how you perceive yourself because if your perception of you doesn't match GOD'S declaration of you, your reality will morph into something hideous; something that reflects the very god whose report you are believing.

Kingdom Thinking

What kind of thinking patterns do the angels of GOD have? They aren't robots, and GOD doesn't control their behaviors. Like us, the angels of GOD have free will to choose whomever they want to serve; they chose JEHOVAH. Now, if you know about Satan and his angels' evictions from Heaven, you should know that a large number of angels that were in Heaven fell with Satan. Nowadays, they are known as devils, demons, and unclean spirits. And just like the angels of GOD, devils have the will to think, plan, and execute. Of course, devils choose to go against GOD; whereas, GOD'S angels work for HIM.

At any given time, we are engaged in our own thoughts. As a matter of fact, the average person has more mental conversations than they have verbal communications. That's because we think about everything we want to do or say, and we also think about the consequences of our actions and words. Additionally, demons are always trying to influence our thoughts by whispering sweet nothings in our spirit. Remember, JESUS was led by the SPIRIT into the wilderness and tested. Satan spoke and JESUS responded. JESUS had the last word, however, because HE is the WORD.

> → **Proverbs 23:7:** For as he thinketh in his heart, so is he: Eat and drink, saith he to thee; but his heart is not with thee.

You are what you think. You are who you believe you are. You are as bad or as good as you believe yourself to be. That's because your thoughts become you. You wear your thoughts from the inside out. That's why Satan is always launching an attack against your mind. He's always trying to change your perception of yourself to match his perception of you. This is bad news for individuals who conceal evil thoughts behind religious smiles. We are as we think and we think as we are. That's why we should get the WORD of GOD in us and continue to meditate on the WORD until we ourselves cannot be separated from the WORD. Right now, many believers speak scriptures, but who they really are is revealed when they are tested. It isn't until they get totally delivered and a total transformation of their minds take place that they can truly say that they are one with CHRIST. To be one with CHRIST doesn't just mean that you're a Christian; it means to be on one accord, to be in total agreement with someone. A husband and wife are one because they have agreed to be one by coming together sexually. A couple isn't married through vows; vows are said to express one's intent to marry and remain together. Marriage occurs once the man and woman have sex. That's why fornication is wrong. In fornication, two people come together as one without GOD'S permission, without the vows, and without the two or three witnesses.

When you were unsaved or freshly saved, if someone was to sneak up on you and scare you, you likely cursed. That's because you were profane. You saw profanity as expressive words designed to get a point across. Whatever we have in us is a part of us; therefore, we are the content of our hearts. If our hearts are wicked, we are wicked. What's in a person will always reveal itself when that person is angry or fearful. For example, when I was growing up, my mother didn't use profanity unless she was extremely angry. We (my siblings and I) could push her buttons for only so long, but when we heard a profane word

Kingdom Thinking

come out of her mouth, we knew that things had just gotten real serious. Whatever we were doing, we stopped and stared at our mother in hopes that the cursed word wasn't about to be followed up with us being ushered into the hallway to get a whooping. Profanity was in my mother's heart, so therefore, she was profane. When I wasn't saved, if something or someone scared me, I would curse. Profanity was in my heart, therefore, I was profane. Profane, according to Merriam-Webster's dictionary means: *to treat (something sacred) with abuse, irreverence, or contempt.* GOD created words; therefore, they are sacred. To speak better, we must learn better.

Kingdom thinking is to think as GOD has created us to think. It is to return to our first love, and learn to speak our original language of love. If you've ever been around someone whose first language is not English, you'll notice that they have an accent. They may speak English proficiently, but they will always speak their own language effeciently. People who are foreigners ordinarily speak limited English; meaning, there are many words that they don't know. They will speak the words that they do know, but anytime you speak with them, they won't likely understand everything you're saying unless you choose your words carefully. If and when they don't understand you, many foreigners will nod their heads as if they do understand you. Kingdom language is the same way. By default, we are citizens of the Kingdom of GOD, and the language of love is our tongue, but we've learned to speak foolishness while in the earth realm. We will always be better at speaking Kingdom than we are at speaking anything else because love is our first language.

Pay attention to children. If you put a bunch of two year old children together in one room, they will likely play with each other. They won't discriminate, nor will they ridicule each other. Instead, they'll play, and then, they'll demonstrate behaviors they've picked up at home. That's because a two year old isn't as learned in the things of the world as he or she is in the things of the Kingdom. A child knows more about love than the average person, and that's why we have to be born again. We teach children the things of the world, but we can learn a lot about love from children. We can learn a lot about the Kingdom just by watching children interact.

Kingdom Thinking

How can we think like an angel of GOD? How can we embrace Kingdom thinking here on earth? Angels are in the presence of GOD daily; therefore, they are in the presence of the WORD of GOD daily. The WORD is not just what they know; it's whom they know. *"In the beginning was the Word, and the Word was with God, and the Word was God" (John 1:1).* The answer is right in our faces, clear as a bright Sunday morning: We simply get to know GOD better by getting into the WORD of GOD. In order to learn a language, you must first be submerged in that language. To learn to speak Kingdom, you must submerge yourself in the language and culture of the Kingdom of GOD.

When I was courting my second ex-husband, I purchased Rosetta Stone so that I could learn to speak French, since French was his first language. In the beginning of our courtship, I studied daily because I was determined to learn the language. I learned words, but not whole phrases. Anytime I would speak something to my then husband, he would tell me that I said it wrong. In most cases, I was putting masculine and feminine verbiage together. Needless to say, I didn't learn French because I wasn't submerged in the language. I learned some French words, but that was it. I wasn't submerged in the language at home because my ex wouldn't speak French unless he was speaking on the phone with someone who spoke French. With me, he spoke English. Additionally, when we lived in Germany, I didn't learn to speak German because I didn't get out the house enough to learn the language. The easiest way to learn a language is to submerge yourself in it.

Germany now has a law that states that anyone who applies for citizenship must learn to speak German. Guess what? The Kingdom of GOD has that same law. You need to speak Kingdom if you want to be a part of the Kingdom. You need to speak love if you want the Kingdom of GOD to be with you as it is in Heaven. You can't be of the world, for the world and in the world, and expect to speak the language of faith. Instead, those who are in the world speak for the world, even those who are in ministry. Pay attention to a minister's following and his words, and you'll identify his first language. In other words, look at the fruit of his ministry and you'll identify the father of his ministry.

What are the benefits of speaking the language of the Kingdom of GOD?

Kingdom Thinking

- You can have whatever you say. Remember, the earth is the LORD'S and the fullness thereof. As a child of GOD, you inherit the Kingdom. You are royalty, and you'll be able to live in and demonstrate the excellency of our GOD, and you will never suffer from lack.
Mark 11:24: *Therefore I say unto you, What things so ever ye desire, when ye pray, believe that ye receive them, and ye shall have them.*
- You'll not only have authority over devils, powers, and principalities; you'll walk in that authority. Every believer has authority over unclean spirits, but few actually have the faith to operate in it.
Luke 10:19: *Behold, I give unto you power to tread on serpents and scorpions, and over all the power of the enemy: and nothing shall by any means hurt you.*
- You'll have peace of mind always and you won't fear anything. Fear is a constrictor, and it slowly squeezes the life out of whomever it inhabits.
2 Timothy 1:7: *For God hath not given us the spirit of fear; but of power, and of love, and of a sound mind.*

- You'll spend your days and nights in the presence of the Almighty GOD. Remember the WORD is GOD, so when you are in the WORD, you are in the presence of GOD.
  Proverbs 8:30-31: Then I was by him, as one brought up with him: and I was daily his delight, rejoicing always before him; rejoicing in the habitable part of his earth; and my delights were with the sons of men.
- You will teach your children to walk in that same authority. A tree always births seed after its own. Whatever you are, you will birth.
  Acts 3:25: *Ye are the children of the prophets, and of the covenant which God made with our fathers, saying unto Abraham, And in thy seed shall all the kindreds of the earth be blessed.*
- The world's system will not affect your house or those of your household. Many believers and leaders are affected by the world's system because they haven't separate themselves from it, but it won't affect you if you learn and apply the WORD of GOD.
  Psalms 91:9-11: *Because thou hast made the LORD, which is my refuge, even the most High, thy habitation; There shall no evil befall*

thee, neither shall any plague come nigh thy dwelling. For he shall give his angels charge over thee, to keep thee in all thy ways.

- You'll have an abundance of wisdom, knowledge, and understanding. As you seek the knowledge of the Kingdom of GOD, GOD will begin to empower you with wisdom and understanding. This threesome is a powerful combo that is more powerful than an army of men, and richer than every man on earth combined.

Proverbs 49:3: *My mouth shall speak of wisdom; and the meditation of my heart shall be of understanding.*

Of course, the benefits of knowing and applying the WORD of GOD are endless, because GOD HIMSELF is without limitations.

Overcoming Procrastination

I lay on the couch with my mind racing. I could feel depression attempting to rise up in my spirit yet again. There were so many things in my spirit to do, but I didn't know where to start. Anytime I thought about stepping outside of my comfort zone to start the businesses GOD told me to start and to write the books GOD told me to write, I felt overwhelmed. That overwhelming feeling was accompanied by a deep sadness and a disappointment in myself. Why was I living a life that wasn't cut out for me? I hated my job, and I was going to work and earning just enough to pay my bills each month. I was the average American. I knew that I shouldn't procrastinate on launching all of the innovative ideas that were constantly running through my mind, but again, I didn't know where to start. At the same time, my heart wasn't right to do many of the things GOD had placed on my life's schedule to do. I had to mature in the things of the LORD; otherwise, my goal would've been to get as much money as I could get my hands on.

Overcoming Procrastination

One day, a commercial came on the television from an invention company. I was going through a divorce, and didn't know how I would pay the mortgage on my home, keep up the monthly utility bills, or pay my car note. I was in desperate need of money, and I was willing to dive into almost any (moral) opportunity that was available.

After watching the commercial, I hurried to my computer and typed in the company's website address. The commercial had stated that the company helps people to bring their inventions to life. I'd had a ton of invention ideas over the years, so I was extremely confident that I could come up with something that would make me an instant success. While filling out the form on the website, I paused at the fields that asked for the invention details because they wanted five invention ideas instead of one. I sat at my computer and tried to think up invention ideas to populate those fields. The first three ideas I had were electronic in nature, and I was very excited about those. I thought they were great ideas, and I was sure the company would select one of them. The last two ideas, on the other hand, seemed hard to think up. I asked myself over and over again what

Overcoming Procrastination

product would be helpful to the average American. At that moment, both of my dogs walked up to me. I had two Siberian Huskies, and they'd pretty much kept me in shape. Suddenly, I remembered one struggle that I often had with my dogs. I walked my Huskies daily, and of course, I had to use two leashes. Being the energetic and unpredictable creatures that they were, my dogs would often run in circles around me, causing me to get tangled up in the leashes. I'd often find myself trying to step out or spin out of their jumbled up leashes, all the while, trying to keep a tight hold on their collars. That's when an idea came in. What if I suggested one leash that could handle multiple dogs? The clamps would rest on long, retractable leash extensions that would allow each dog enough room to wander, but would also allow the dogs' handlers to adjust the leash. I was excited about the idea, but I was still pretty much sold on my electronic ideas, including a fish tank that would double as a wide screen television.

I input my ideas into the fields, and within a day or less, I received a call from one of their agents. He said he liked two of my ideas, but to my surprise, it wasn't the fish tank or the other electronic ideas. He

Overcoming Procrastination

liked the leash and the other idea I'd come up with on a whim (not sure what it was anymore). I was surprised, but I didn't care; after all, he was the professional. I was looking for a quick (and lazy) way to earn a million bucks, and coughing up invention ideas seemed like a great idea. The whole time, I still had those assignments in my heart that GOD had given me, but because of the way I thought back then, I delayed HIS will in search of an easier way. I listened intently as the agent told me about my options, but the only thing that I could really hear was that I'd need to send them over seven hundred dollars to start the process. I didn't have seven hundred bucks to spare. I couldn't even afford to pay the bills I had coming in, so I definitely couldn't consider parting with seven hundred bucks. I thanked the agent and told him that I'd be in touch if my financial situation changed. As we hung up the phone, I realized that I'd just given away several ideas, two of which the agent really liked. What would he do with those ideas? Would he just forget about them and toss them into the trash? Somehow, I knew better.

A year later, I was watching television when an infomercial came on. Some company was introducing my idea: The retractable leash that held multiple dogs. I stood to my feet in shock. Had the company stolen my idea, or had someone else stumbled across that idea? Of course, I elected to believe that I'd just handed away a million dollar idea to someone else, and hadn't got anything in return but a story to tell my future grand kids.

After that, I went back to my couch in depression, and I continued to battle against whom I was deep down inside, but eventually, GOD prevailed in my life.

Depression is nothing more than the reaction your mind gives when you suppress a GOD-given assignment. It is the desire to be something or someone other than who you were called to be. It is your inner-man crying from within the prison you've created for him. Depression is your soul's way of saying you're going in the wrong direction. It is when your spirit man is speaking, but his voice is drowned out by the sounds of doubt, worry, fear, and the cares of the world. Depression is an allergic reaction to whatever you're exposing your mind, soul, and spirit to.

The average believer has many talents. The average

believer has buried many of his or her talents. How did they bury their talents? They buried them by not utilizing them, or by perverting those talents and using them for the world. This means that something that was supposed to empower GOD'S people is now being prostituted to the world, or it's being suppressed. For this reason, the average believer is depressed. That's because we, as believers, were not supposed to work for this world; we were nominated by GOD to create jobs and the world was supposed to work for us.

What happens when you suppress a talent? Your talent is what separates you from the rest. It is what makes you extraordinary, but whenever you suppress (or bury) a talent, you give up the extra to become ordinary. An average person is only average because that person has rejected whom they were to fit into the world's system. The world's system creates robots, and encourages people to behave, think, and reason in the same manner that their leaders behave, think, and reason. Most people choose to be average because it takes faith, courage, and perseverance to stand out in a world that shuns anyone who attempts to stand out from it. The world also celebrates, and sometimes worships, anyone who's successfully gotten through all of the obstacles they've thrown at them. So, if you're a talented singer, and you've overcome your condescending kinfolks, refused to be discouraged by your wrongful termination, refused to be defined by your lack of education, and you've lasted through several seasons of depression without losing your mind or your desire to sing, you'll be considered extraordinary. That's because the world tries any and everyone who dares to stand out, but it'll celebrate any and everyone who refuses to be boxed in.

Additionally, when you suppress a talent or delay unearthing it, you'll find yourself always feeling as if there was something you were supposed to do or something you are called to do. You may begin to see your assignment as something that GOD intends to give you in the future, but in truth, your assignments are already locked up on the inside of you. Those assignments are unlocked season by season as you continue to advance in HIS WORD and HIS will. You'll find that whenever you begin to utilize the talents that GOD has given you, and you use them for HIS glory, you'll be successful at what you do because it's what you were created to do. Failure means that you are failing at being someone else or completing an assignment that was not your own.

All too often, I've met men and women who weren't sure who they were. Like most believers, they'd become ensnared in a system that dictated what they were to do with most of their time. They knew that they had callings on their lives. Many of them knew what their callings were, but they delayed answering those calls because they felt they weren't financially, mentally, or spiritually prepared to handle their assignments. The average believer said they needed more money to finally do what GOD told them to do. In other words, they were trying to climb a mountain backwards.

→ **Proverbs 18:** A man's gift maketh room for him, and bringeth him before great men.

Here's the thing: You can't be a success if you're refusing to be who you are because being yourself is what you'll be successful at doing. Your success isn't in learning multiple skills; your success is being who GOD has created and skilled you to be. For example,

Overcoming Procrastination

I have friends who have beautiful singing voices. They can sing beautifully without much effort. If they were to use their talents and build a career with those talents, they'd be successful if they didn't allow the trials of life or the cares of the world to run them back into their comfort zones. They could go before great men with their voices. As for me, it would be better for me (and the great men) if I stayed at home with my singing voice. When GOD was handing out talents, I was obviously in a different line, but the point is: My singing voice is not pleasant. So, it would be foolish (and humorous) of me to try and launch a singing career. I can't be like my friends because I have a different assignment to fulfill in the LORD, and my identity is directly linked to my assignment. If I were to try and become a singer, I'd likely suffer from depression because I'd have to suppress who I really am to be whomever I'm trying to be.

Your gift will make room for you... period. No one else's gift will make room for you; your gift will make room for you, and your gift will bring you before great men. What you'll find is that you've likely been suppressing your gifts, but there are plenty of people who've tried to utilize your gifts for their own gain.

Overcoming Procrastination

These people include your family members, your co-workers, your friends, and your superiors. So, if you are a great writer, you'll likely have people who ask you to do their homework for them, review their job assignments, or write whatever materials they need written. That's because they see your talents, even if you don't. At the same time, when your talents are hidden, you won't see the value in them, so you'll allow people to use them at their own will.

Procrastination is the first step towards depression. Think of it this way: What if a dog refused its identity and began to meow? He's a dog, so he's supposed to be barking and hanging out with other dogs, but because he's having an identity crisis, he's meowing and trying to hang out with cats. When he's in the presence of other dogs, he's often attacked or chased, and when he's in the presence of cats, he's often avoided or hissed at. Imagine what he would feel like. He'd be sad because he would not only be confused about his identity, but he'd also be lonely. Let's say that the cats accepted him into their group. He'd still be lonely because none of the cats would be able to identify with him. That's how depression works in most people. A person who's depressed has a lot on his or her mind that he or she is trying to suppress, and they can't find anyone who can relate to them. Sure, they can find plenty of depressed people, but they'd have trouble finding people who knew why they were depressed.

One thing you'll notice is that a person who is abrupt, unapologetic, and without tact is oftentimes successful. We view their curtness as them being rude, disrespectful, and insensitive, but in many cases, they are simply people who've learned how much weight procrastination and expectation can put on a person. So, if you walk up to the owner of a chain of companies, and you told him your great idea, he'd likely shoot down your idea without putting too much thought into it. Of course, you'd be offended, but that's the least of his problems; instead, that would be your own problem. That's because he understands that he has the weight of running his company on his shoulders. He can't take your idea and the other five thousand ideas that have been thrown at him within the last six months, and promise to get back with you and everyone else. That's a job in itself. He's learned what works and what doesn't work, and he's learned that promising people that he'd

Overcoming Procrastination

review their ideas could cost him too much of his time. Additionally, it could serve as a foundation for future lawsuits. What if someone who's already working for him had already pitched that idea? What if he suddenly came up with that idea on his own? If he'd allowed you and others to pitch ideas at him, he'd likely be sued if he were to implement any of those ideas without giving credit to the people who believe that those ideas are original to them. Let's go back to my leash idea. I couldn't sue the company who created and marketed the leash because I can't truly say that they stole my idea. Maybe someone else had a couple of dogs that were giving them the same problems that my dogs were giving me. Maybe that person had come up with the same idea that I'd come up with. It's not impossible nor is it far fetched.

Therefore, the owner of a chain of companies cannot arrange meetings with everyone who says they have a great idea. After listening to a person pitch an idea at them, they'll likely thank the person, but tell them that they are currently not in the market for that particular product or service.

To procrastinate is to delay your purpose; it is to put

off being who you are because you think that you can find success in developing your own identity or because you're afraid to be as talented as you are. The fear of success is more common than most people are aware of. As a matter of fact, the large majority of people fear success, even though they want to be rich. What's the difference? Most people don't want to go before great men; they don't want to stand out. They simply want the riches that accompany success, but not the problems nor the recognition that accompanies success. This means that the average person wants to get rich to consume their wealth upon themselves, but has no desire to give GOD the glory because they fear what they'll lose in the process. Many people won't do what GOD told them to do because they are afraid that they'll be successful at it. They know that being successfully talented means their lives would change, and that life as they know it would never be the same. Yet, they aren't willing to come out of their comfort zones because the average person hates change. As a matter of fact, most of the times when someone says they are going through a trial, what they're really saying is they're going through an unwanted change. They're saying that they are in the process of resisting

Overcoming Procrastination

something that's trying to become a part of their lives or their realities. Sometimes, the change is good; other times, the change is not so good, but either way, they are resistant to the change.

How can you overcome procrastination?
- Further educate yourself about procrastination.
- Ask the LORD to show you your talents once again.
- Unearth those talents.
- Get busy in your talents, and be sure to stay busy in them. In the beginning, you probably won't be at an expert level, but if you stay consistent, you'll be better than good at whatever you're talented at.
- Look for baby killers, and remove them from your life immediately. Your talents are your babies, and there are many people who will seek to destroy those babies before they're born. Some people will attempt to discourage you, while others may attempt to take those talents from you. Pay attention to the people in your life. As you get in the will of GOD, many of the people whose seasons are up in your life or who were never supposed to be in your life will

begin to oppose you. Don't get angry; they are simply identifying themselves.
- Create a business plan or a planner.
- Invest money in whatever it is you are talented at doing. Remember, being talented doesn't necessarily mean being immediately on the expert level. Most people value their money, so by investing the very thing you value (money) into something else, you'll automatically transfer the value of your money into whatever it is that you've purchased. For example, if you're talented at singing, you could buy song editing equipment, studio equipment, or microphones. You could also invest in getting a website, logo, voice coaching, or anything that assists with your singing career. By investing in your vocal talents, you'll begin to value your talents more; therefore, you'll use them more.
- Distance yourself from your slothful friends. Mentalities are like viruses; they are contagious, and if you continually expose yourself to them, you'll eventually become a victim of the way you think. During the time that I'd gone through bouts of depression, I had a friend who used to come to my house, and she

Overcoming Procrastination

was extremely slothful. Before long, I began to pick up on her ways, even sleeping throughout the day. When GOD removed her from my life, I got my energy back.

- Remember, it takes 17-21 days to establish a habit. Don't become disheartened if you aren't successful at breaking bad habits immediately. Obstacles have met everyone who has attempted to change, and many have failed at change, only to get back up and try again. Those who are successful at changing are usually the ones who refused to change their minds about making a change to their lives. They're the ones who didn't let falling off the horse keep them from getting back in the saddle.
- Penalize yourself for every day that you don't do something to break your habit of procrastination. Be sure to create a life's menu (planner), print it off, and commit to following it. For every day that you fail, penalize yourself.
- Make sure that whatever you do, you do for the glory of GOD. When you do something for yourself, you'll likely get tired of doing it and settle for something else, but when you do

something for GOD, you're not going to want to fail at it.

- **Galatians 6:9**: And let us not be weary in well doing: for in due season we shall reap, if we faint not.
- **Proverbs 19:21**: There are many devices in a man's heart; nevertheless the counsel of the LORD, that shall stand.
- **Matthew 14:30:** For the kingdom of heaven is as a man traveling into a far country, who called his own servants, and delivered unto them his goods. And unto one he gave five talents, to another two, and to another one; to every man according to his several ability; and straightway took his journey. Then he that had received the five talents went and traded with the same, and made them other five talents. And likewise he that had received two, he also gained other two. But he that had received one went and digged in the earth, and hid his lord's money. After a long time the lord of those servants cometh, and reckoneth with them. And so he that had received five talents came and brought other five talents, saying, Lord,

Overcoming Procrastination

thou deliveredst unto me five talents: behold, I have gained beside them five talents more. His lord said unto him, Well done, thou good and faithful servant: thou hast been faithful over a few things, I will make thee ruler over many things: enter thou into the joy of thy lord. He also that had received two talents came and said, Lord, thou deliveredst unto me two talents: behold, I have gained two other talents beside them. His lord said unto him, Well done, good and faithful servant; thou hast been faithful over a few things, I will make thee ruler over many things: enter thou into the joy of thy lord. Then he which had received the one talent came and said, Lord, I knew thee that thou art an hard man, reaping where thou hast not sown, and gathering where thou hast not strawed: And I was afraid, and went and hid thy talent in the earth: lo, there thou hast that is thine. His lord answered and said unto him, Thou wicked and slothful servant, thou knewest that I reap where I sowed not, and gather where I have not strawed: Thou oughtest therefore to have put my money to the exchangers, and then at my coming I should have received mine own with usury. Take therefore the talent from him, and give it unto him which hath ten talents. For unto every one that hath shall be given, and he shall have abundance: but from him that hath not shall be taken away even that which he hath. And cast ye the unprofitable servant into outer darkness: there shall be weeping and gnashing of teeth.

The Power of a Made Up Mind

Anytime I counsel a brokenhearted woman who is suffering because of a recent breakup, one of the things I encourage her to do is to make up her mind in relation to her estranged partner. I encourage her to decide what she wants and to settle it in her mind. That's because one obstacle that slows down and worsens the grieving process is uncertainty. That's when a person isn't sure which direction they want to go in, but they are being rushed by their emotions to make a decision. After a breakup, most men and women are still mentally in a relationship with the person they've just broken up with. The time immediately after a breakup is usually a time when both parties pour out more words than they allow in because they are both trying to get their points across. After one of the parties involved ceases to communicate with the other party, both individuals start considering what their estranged partners said, as well as considering other events of the relationship that led to its downfall. This means that they are still mentally in that relationship, even though they've physically exited it. During this stage, it is never wise for either party to enter a new relationship because (1) they aren't fully healed, and (2) they haven't reached the stage of acceptance.

I've noticed that almost every brokenhearted woman I've counseled was dealing with the same thing: uncertainty. They'd already declared that the relationships were over, but they had yet to exit those relationships mentally. So, they mulled over every old or new revelation they could think of in their attempts to get answers. They had many questions, and they felt robbed because their ex-partners weren't making it easy for them to get the answers they felt they needed. Why did they need answers? The truth is: They hadn't quite made up their minds about the status of their relationships. They weren't sure if they wanted those relationships to be over. They wanted to have a long, heart-to-heart conversation with their ex-partners, but they knew that those meetings would likely never happen, and if they did, they knew that their ex-partners would likely be dishonest. Because of this, they dedicated most of their time to looking for the answers they felt their exes were hiding from them. Many of these women said they needed closure to finally be at peace with the breakups, but in truth, closure is oftentimes just an excuse to "talk about it." It's just another way for the party who hasn't let go of the relationship to get the answers they need to stay in that relationship. It is oftentimes an attempt for them to pull on the heartstrings of their estranged lovers as well, hoping that they can reconcile. For this reason, I discourage a woman from pursuing a conversation that her ex doesn't want to have, because she'll likely go into that conversation certain that she's about to reconcile with her ex, but oftentimes, leaves the conversation even more hurt and bitter than she was before she went in.

To be confused simply means to be undecided. To be confused means that you have two or more options to consider, and you're uncertain of which option you want to take. Of course, being undecided equates to being unstable in your thinking. *"A double minded*

The Power of a Made Up Mind

man is unstable in all his ways" (James 1:8). Anytime a person is undecided, that person absolutely does not have peace. Peace is a state of mind that accompanies certainty, but peace eludes a double-minded man. It doesn't matter how big or small an event or decision is if a person has not made up their mind about that event or decision, they will not have peace about it. Oftentimes, when we have decisions that we can delay, we tuck those decisions away for later, and we become irritated with anyone who attempts to bring those decisions to the forefront or anyone who attempts to rush us into making a decision. Needless to say, however, delaying a decision does not make it easier; it simply gives us more time to look at and consider our options. It also gives us more time to worry, doubt, or even believe.

There is absolute power behind a made-up mind. There is peace in a made-up mind; not just a changed mind, but a mind that's settled. This means that once we make a decision in our hearts, we can then rest and deal with everything that comes with that decision. It doesn't matter if a decision is good or bad,

The Power of a Made Up Mind

a person who's made a decision will find peace, unless, of course, they are uncertain about the decisions they've made. Let's revisit the topic of the women I've counseled. Many of them had lost their lovers to other women, and they were hurt, angry, and confused. They didn't understand why they were hurting so badly, while their runaway lovers seemed to be happy, content, and at peace. The truth is: Their ex-lovers had made up their minds. They'd decided that they wanted to build or continue a relationship with their new lovers, so they were able to walk away from their past lovers without shedding so much as a tear. Even though they'd betrayed a person, they found peace in a made-up mind. It goes without saying, however, that anytime a person makes a bad decision, that decision will slowly begin to unravel when it's challenged by truth. In many cases of betrayal, the betrayer eventually has a change of heart and ends up back in a state of confusion. That's because even though there is peace in a made-up mind, the truth will always challenge our decisions.

What decisions have you put off? What decisions are

The Power of a Made Up Mind

you struggling to make? All too often, we know what GOD wants us to do, but we delay making those decisions because of what we believe we're losing by making those decisions. That's why GOD said that HE is not the author of confusion, and of course, if HE'S not the author of confusion, Satan is. GOD simply tells us what we need to do, but Satan often tells us what we want to do. So, we look at what GOD says, and we can't see what's ahead of that decision; all we can see is the pain or the emptiness we believe we will endure after making that decision. When we look at what Satan offers, we often see everything we want ahead of that decision. The enemy will often present us with what we want, but behind everything he gives, there is a price to pay, and oftentimes, we can't afford to pay that price. What GOD gives to us is oftentimes free, but to acquire those blessings, we have to walk away from the things and the people that GOD has told us to walk away from. This undoubtedly is for our own protection because GOD sees what we do not see, and HE knows what we do not know.

Every decision first starts off as a question, but when

we learn to trust GOD, we learn to take HIS WORD to heart. At the same time, when we learn to trust GOD, we learn to just let HIM tell us which way we should go with any decisions we find ourselves facing. Sometimes, GOD will tell us to take the unfamiliar paths that we don't want to take, but in obeying HIM, we'll always find out why HE sent us in those directions.

Let's take divorce, for example. If you were ever married and considering a divorce, chances are, your mind had changed about your spouse at some point in that marriage. Before you made up your mind to separate yourself from your spouse, you would have gone through a series of events that changed your mind about the spouse. Once your mind was changed, you saw your spouse differently and you wanted to divorce the person they'd become or revealed themselves to be. You were once in love with who you thought your spouse was, but once they started changing or revealing who they really were, you changed your mind about them. Before your mind changed, however, you did try to encourage them to

The Power of a Made Up Mind

change those behaviors you believed to be affecting your marriage. But if they refused to be whom you wanted or thought them to be, you changed your mind about them. After your mind had been changed, you then began to consider the alternatives. You considered staying in the marriage with the person your spouse has revealed him or herself to be, and you've considered exiting the marriage. Once you made up your mind as to which decision you wanted to make, you found peace in that decision. Sure, your heart may have been broken, but you had peace because you'd made up your mind.

There is power in a made-up mind. As a matter of fact, if you were to take everything that you are unsure of, pray about it, and make the decision that GOD told you to make, you would find yourself in absolute peace and joy. Many of the obstacles that Satan throws at you aren't necessarily designed to bring you down instantly; they are designed to confuse you, get you into a state of uncertainty, and bring you down slowly and painfully. Once you're there, the enemy will then continue his assault against

The Power of a Made Up Mind

your mind by giving you imaginations of all the horrible things that he says could happen to you if you were to obey GOD. He continues to show you alternatives to consider; all the while, accusing you of being double-minded before the LORD. Worry and doubt are both environments that the enemy thrives in, and that's why he's always looking to attack your mind. But when you make up your mind to do what GOD said to do and don't consider what the enemy is saying, he loses his power against you, and all he can do is watch helplessly as GOD continues to bless, lead, and prosper you.

A changed mind is great, but a made-up mind is even better. How so? The enemy can always get a person to reconsider what he or she has said and get that person to change his or her mind, but a person with a made-up mind is unmovable.

The Depth of Understanding

Your reality is whatever manifests itself as real to you. Your reality is your understanding, and your understanding is what you know to be true coupled with what you believe to be true. Knowledge and understanding births perception, and if we don't have Godly knowledge or understanding, we will have ungodly perceptions of ourselves and others.

I was talking with a woman one day, when she began to tell me about some of the people whom she'd believed had tried to do witchcraft on her. She believed that a lot of people were out to get her, and that some were even out to kill her. As I listened to her, I immediately recognized a spirit that was at work in her. I spoke with another woman who believed that Muslims were hacking into her computer and making the screen smaller in an attempt to cripple her ministry. I'd even spoken with a woman who believed the government was after her. She believed that the government was tapping her phone, staking out her

The Depth of Understanding

house, and scanning her brain. Now, every one of these women were not only in ministry, but they were also in leadership! In the world, they refer to this spirit as a condition called "schizophrenia", but as believers, we know that it is a demonic spirit. Truthfully, I've spoken with numerous people in the church who had that same spirit in operation within them, and I have come to understand why GOD said to try the spirits. *"Beloved, believe not every spirit, but try the spirits whether they are of God: because many false prophets are gone out into the world" (1 John 4:1).*

Just a few years back, I would have easily believed every one of those women were women of GOD because I thought that everyone who had a ministry, said they believed in JESUS CHRIST, and had people following them was actually a genuine Christian. GOD used many of those (or similar) experiences to get me to stop leaning to my own understanding (the lazy way out) and actually trying the spirit by the spirit to see if it is of GOD.

The Depth of Understanding

What had happened to these women? How could they come to a point where they lived in fear of events that were clearly unreal? We can sum the answer up in one word: understanding.

It had all started with an imagination that had not been cast down. For example, we often see things that we can add together, create theories, and then, sum those theories up as truths. In most cases, when we do this, we are either upset with someone or we're trying to figure something out on our own. So, as human beings, we'll take what we do know and apply our own reasoning to it. Whenever we don't have the answers, we'll start filling in the blanks with whatever makes sense to us. After a while, a picture begins to come together. Before long, we've developed a logical-sounding theory. Once we accept those theories as truth, they become our understandings or beliefs, and they will begin to shape our minds, perceptions, and realities. Every understanding that we have serves as a foundation or building block for a new imagination followed by a new understanding. In this, you'll notice that GOD'S WORD was not followed.

The Depth of Understanding

Please review the following scriptures:

→ **Proverbs 3:5: Trust in the LORD with all thine heart; and lean not unto thine own understanding.**

In this scripture, we see that the LORD commands us to trust in HIM, and HE made it clear that depending on our own understanding was the polar opposite of trusting HIM. Why did HE tell us not to depend on our own understanding? Because our understanding comes from our hearts and not HIS. We oftentimes use our hearts as trash cans for imaginations that were not cast down. Those imaginations become beliefs or they shape our beliefs if they are pondered or considered for too long. Each belief that we have serves as a foundation for other beliefs, and anything we place on top of those beliefs will always be contaminated by the foundation that it stands on.

→ **Jeremiah 17:9: The heart is deceitful above all things, and desperately wicked: who can know it?**

The Depth of Understanding

Again, the heart is oftentimes used as a trash can for imaginations. Any thought that comes in our mind is a thought that's trying to get into our hearts. Whatever we don't believe, we will likely instantly reject; we won't even consider it. To consider means to mentally pick something apart with the intent of observing it. But there are and were many things that came to our minds that we never really resolved because we hadn't decided if what we were observing was the truth or a lie. So, in an attempt to get our peace back, we filed those things at the back of our minds and left them there. Of course, our imaginations kept vomiting those thoughts back up in our minds, but because we didn't know what to make of those thoughts, we kept filing them away until they became beliefs. You'll notice that there may be some situation going on in your life or someone else's life that you'd never put too much thought into because you couldn't figure it out, but the minute someone came to you and brought up that conversation, you had a definite answer about that person or situation. Even though you hadn't thought much about it, your mind had been made up in relation to that situation. You were likely

The Depth of Understanding

shocked at your response because it was the first time you'd said it out loud or even pondered it for more than ten seconds. What happened was, your understanding filtered that situation, and you subconsciously made up your mind about the situation without even consciously considering it. That's because the mind is powerful enough to take what's in it, filter it through our understanding, and bring it to rest in our beliefs. The women I spoke of had tried to take what they saw or what they thought they saw and they considered whatever the enemy had put in their minds. They didn't rebuke the thoughts or try the spirits; instead, they took the understandings that they already had and filtered their thoughts or perceptions through those understandings.

→ **2 Corinthians 10:5:** Casting down imaginations, and every high thing that exalteth itself against the knowledge of God, and bringing into captivity every thought to the obedience of Christ.

The Depth of Understanding

The truth is: We all deal with evil imaginations, and most of us wish there was some type of button that we could push to shut them off. Evil imaginations can be haunting, and sometimes, terrifying. At the same time, some evil imaginations are entertaining, funny, and seemingly good. We'll oftentimes entertain those imaginations when they present to us something that we want. For example, if you're a single man who has a crush on a particular woman, you likely won't cast down positive imaginations about her. You'll probably envision yourself kissing her, holding her hand, or even bedding her. If you don't cast the thought down immediately, that thought will find its way into your heart and become a belief. Before long, you may find yourself thinking you're destined to be with that woman, and you may obsessively pursue (stalk) her because you allowed an evil imagination to penetrate your heart, thus, giving the enemy access to your heart.

With the women in question, those thoughts weren't cast down; instead, they were pondered and then, accepted as truth.

The Depth of Understanding

→ **Psalm 55:22:** Cast thy burden upon the LORD, and he shall sustain thee: he shall never suffer the righteous to be moved.

Worry and doubt should never be found in us, and wrath should be cast out before the sun sets each day. Worry, doubt, and anger wages war against our minds, and they often set the stage for new thoughts to come in. Think about a woman who's married to an adulterous man. She will often carry the burden of what her husband is doing because she feels the impact of it every day that she's with him. GOD told her to cast that burden on HIM, but because she's emotionally involved and hurting, she'll likely carry that burden and try to resolve it on her own. Sure, she may pray and ask GOD to intervene, but because she's being moved by the burden on her heart, she has not given GOD the green light to move on her behalf. Additionally, GOD doesn't intervene; HE simply concludes a situation by speaking to it. Intervention means to assist, but GOD doesn't want us to share in HIS glory; HE wants us to be still, know that HE is GOD, and witness HIM bring our situations

The Depth of Understanding

into submission to HIS WORD. In her attempt to protect herself, the betrayed wife will expose herself to more pain; the very pain in which the LORD wanted to protect her from. Because she's not trusting in the LORD, she will not be stable or at peace because stability and peace only come from GOD.

In life, we are confronted by various situations that we don't want to face, and each of those situations either stand above our faith, at eye-level with our faith, or beneath our faith. If we believe GOD, those situations are small to us and are immediately overcome. Even though they may still be manifested in the realm of the earth, we still believe GOD and we see those situations as dead. If we don't believe GOD, those situations may tower over our faith, and we will likely resort to using our own devices in an attempt to bring those situations down. Finally, if we're at eye-level with those situations, we'll likely throw scriptures at what we see, not understanding that we still need faith to claim the victories given to us through CHRIST JESUS. In a case like this, we'll likely keep being revisited by the same problems because we're

The Depth of Understanding

throwing scriptures at them with no faith to propel those scriptures; meaning, we know what the WORD says, but we don't believe what the WORD says. Anytime a believer knows the WORD but doesn't believe the WORD, that person will become a faithless scripture chanter. That person will often host religious rituals using scriptural repetition, many words, and much shouting, but those rituals are powerless because the person hosting those rituals is faithless.

Our understanding has a depth to it, and it is usually rooted in the foundation that it stands on. For example, if you understand the sky to be blue, you would have first had to understand how to identify the color blue. You would have also known that the firmament above you is called a sky; therefore, before you concluded that the sky was blue, you understood what a sky was and what the color blue looked like. One understanding stood on the other to bring about a conclusion. This also means that if you are full of lies, each layer of lies will have to be challenged by the truth, proven to be lies, and destroyed. Once one

The Depth of Understanding

layer is removed, whatever foundation it was standing on must go through that very same process of being challenged by the truth, proven to be lies, and destroyed.

Truthfully, many of the conditions we refer to as mental illnesses are nothing more than demonic possessions or demonic suggestions. Many people don't take what pops up in their minds before the LORD, and if you continue to believe everything that rises up in your head, you will slowly deteriorate until you start thinking, believing, and reasoning like a mad man.

Nowadays, I don't just allow anyone to pray for me or to speak into my life, because I need to know the spirit that's behind or in them. I need to know whom they are hearing from, so they don't speak something into my life that GOD didn't speak into my life. Most of the people that I've met who were in leadership and obviously dealing with what some would refer to as mental illnesses, had people who followed their ministries. Most of them referred to themselves as

The Depth of Understanding

deliverance ministers, and most of them practiced laying hands (impartations) on other believers. Undoubtedly, the people who were following their ministries did not consult the LORD first; instead, they simply walked into a church, liked the way the preacher was preaching, and decided to join that church. Some may even say that GOD told them to join that church, but we have to be careful always and remember that Satan disguises himself as an angel of light. Don't be so surprised that the enemy would try to impersonate GOD. That's why we see so many false prophets and apostles rising up, and we see accounts of people claiming to be JESUS CHRIST. We have to try the spirits by the spirit; otherwise, we'll end up unknowingly in submission to demonic spirits.

One day, I decided to move my personal website from a flash hosting site to a WordPress site because flash sites can't be viewed from mobile devices unless the viewer has a flash program installed on his or her mobile device. I was still using my ex-husband's surname as my own, and of course, I wanted to transition out of that name. I knew that people would

The Depth of Understanding

look for me at my old domain name, so I didn't want to get rid of the domain name completely, but I did want a new domain. From there, I had to make a decision: I could have my old domain redirected to a new domain, or I could create an intro site where viewers would find themselves on nothing more than an intro page. That intro page would have a link that led to my new website. Of course, the second method required more work and more money, but it would have the best impact because it would inform viewers that my site's link had been changed. The intro site would act as a portal from one site to the next. It would catch all of my website traffic, give them the information they need, and offer them a way into the new site. That's how understanding works. It serves as a bridge between one belief and the next. Anytime understanding is rooted in the truth, you will be given the opportunity to cross over into new understandings, and you'll be led to this bridge by whatever you have going on in your life at any given time. At the same time, misguided understandings often serve as demonic access portals, giving unclean spirits the information, foundations, and environments

The Depth of Understanding

they'll need to continue their evil campaigns against the truth. This would give the enemy the ability to catch every truth that attempted to enter into your hearts, take that truth through your darkened understanding, and abort that truth while it's still in your mind. In other words, a WORD-starved heart will always be a demon's cubicle.

What you understand is a foundation that will contaminate or fertilize any new information that comes into your mind or heart. For this reason, it is vital that you not only know what the WORD says, but you should understand what the WORD says. Knowledge without understanding is unfruitful. Think of it this way: There are many people who know how to steer a car and keep it on the road, but they do not understand the signs on the road. Simply knowing how to steer a car is not enough to declare yourself a driver if you don't understand the traffic signs. Knowing how to maneuver a vehicle is only half of what you need in order to drive. You also have to learn traffic signs and the rules of the road; otherwise, you'll likely harm or kill yourself or someone else.

The Depth of Understanding

Finally, you will have to be licensed to drive to be considered a legal driver.

Whatever you understand will manifest itself as your reality and set the stage for new understandings, so if you want to change your life, you need to change your understanding. If your understanding does not match up with the WORD of GOD, it needs to be uprooted layer by layer until the very foundation of those lies is revealed and destroyed. That way, you can allow the WORD of GOD to be the foundation of your beliefs, and you won't suffer from paranoia, doubt, or fear; instead, you will enjoy the peace that surpasses all understanding.

The Power of Repetition

Generally, it takes 17 to 21 days of consistency to establish a habit, and it usually takes that same amount of time to break a habit. Needless to say, most people have repetitious behaviors they engage in, and many of these behaviors have been a part of their routines for years. Howbeit, the average person refuses to establish new habits, because new habits always pose as a threat to old habits. Our old habits are the very things that have created the comfort zones we've come to enjoy, so by denouncing old habits, we know and understand that we will go through a period of uncertainty and discomfort. For this reason, the average person will likely remain average for the rest of his or her life, but those who usually break the molds of repetition oftentimes find success. Most people who dare to float above the "average" label are ridiculed, persecuted, judged, and questioned by average-minded people about their choices to do whatever it is that sets them apart from

The Power of Repetition

others. Then again, there are many people who are above average-minded, but the fear of standing out keeps them from revealing what they fear others may see as their "super-powers". People like this are oftentimes surrounded by friends and family members who openly ridicule anyone who's not like themselves. For example, I grew up in a poor family, and of course, I grew up in poor neighborhoods. What I noticed was that many of the children in some of the areas I'd lived in were secretly talented, but they were ashamed of their gifts. When I'd questioned them about keeping their gifts a secret, many of those children said that they had family members, neighbors, or classmates who'd ridiculed them about their talents. Some of their parents had even ridiculed them. They got tired of being the butt of jokes, so they did what they knew would keep them from standing out: They learned to fit in. After a while, most of those children had begun to see their gifts as curses. They stopped using their talents, and before long, they had a habit of being who they'd learned to be, and they had a habit of concealing their real identities.

The Power of Repetition

Whatever you are, you've learned to be through the act of repetition. For example, you learned to eat with a spoon because you consistently picked up a spoon and ate with it. More than likely, as a toddler you weren't very good at holding or eating with a spoon, but you didn't give up. Your parents had stopped feeding you or you got tired of them feeding you, so you started trying to manage the spoon on your own. Like most toddlers, you probably spilled a lot of food on the floor in your attempts to feed yourself. But after a while, you'd learned to be a skilled spoon handler, and now, handling a spoon is second nature to you.

For every new thing we engage in, we come in as unskilled, but with consistency, we finally reach the skilled level. Some people reach the expert level because they dedicate more time and have more passion about whatever it is they are engaging in than others. So, if you wanted to learn how to create software, for example, you would have to start at the bottom (unskilled) and work your way up until you'd either become a skilled software creator or a professional software creator.

The Power of Repetition

What's the point? Anything on earth that you want to be, you can be if you dedicate time to doing it, and don't give up. Additionally, your talents are already inside you, and your talents are easily identified because whatever you are talented with, you will be passionate about. For example, I've written over twenty books (currently) in less than five years because I'm passionate about writing. Anytime I teach a writing class, I can always tell who's a talented writer as opposed to who is just writing for the sake of getting the "author" label. A talented (supernaturally gifted by GOD) student will always be passionate about writing, and they'll oftentimes go above and beyond each assignment given to them. But the ones who weren't gifted to write are oftentimes easily offended, and getting a completed assignment out of them is like pulling teeth. That's because whatever we're not gifted with, we won't be passionate about unless we're knowledgeable about it.

Repetition can be good and repetition can be bad. Habitually keeping your house clean is a good habit, but habitually living in disarray is a bad habit. People who live in disarray have done so for a long time. Even though their living quarters is in shambles, they've learned to function in their homes and will likely become offended with anyone who attempts to clean or organize their homes. Disorganization is their normal; whereas, your normal may be found in a well-organized space. People who shower daily do so because it's a habit, and they won't feel at peace if they go without showering. Showering daily is their normal. People who do not shower daily don't do so because poor hygiene is a habit for them, and their peace is only disturbed when they are forced or coerced into taking a shower. That's because poor hygiene is their normal.

Can people with bad habits break those habits and establish new habits? Of course they can. In order to break a habit, a person has to repeatedly and purposely do something other than the routines they're accustomed to doing. For example, if a man wanted to stop smoking, he would have to consistently reject cigarettes for 17-21 days. In order for him to do this, he'd likely use a distraction to keep

The Power of Repetition

his mind off smoking. That's the purpose of many of the patches and programs designed for people who want to stop smoking. The makers of these programs and patches understand that the people who buy their products will need something to distract and soothe them for 17-21 days. It's not the medication or the therapy that heals the smoker; it's the forming of a new habit that heals the smoker. The programs, patches, and therapy distract and educate the smoker, but they don't heal him. Many scientists who've created products to help smokers to stop smoking looked for non-addictive products that could mimic the behaviors of nicotine, without the harmful effects of nicotine. The goal was to get the smokers to make a habit of smoking something that was less harmful and less addictive than cigarettes.

The easiest way to build a habit is to create a month-long schedule for yourself. On the schedule, you should incorporate what it is that you want to make a habit of. This means that you will have to rearrange your life to allow a new habit in. To make this more effective, you should establish your intentions in the

The Power of Repetition

presence of two or three witnesses, and you should set up steep penalties for the days that you do not comply with your schedule. The penalties should be of greater value to you than your daily routine. For example, I had a habit of eating bread with every meal I ate. I also had a habit of going to McDonald's every other day, and I had sodas almost daily. I ate one meal a day, and snacked for the rest of the day, and I would go weeks without drinking any pure water. Instead, I'd drink sodas, tea, and juices each and everyday. It's no surprise that I picked up weight in that lifestyle. I didn't eat much fruit, and I didn't exercise a lot.

One day, I stepped on the scale and learned that I'd gained another eight pounds within a month's time. I was devastated, but I knew that it was past time for me to do something about my eating habits. So, I created a daily planner using Microsoft Word, and in that planner, I said that for thirty days, I would not:

- Eat McDonald's
- Eat any white bread
- Drink any sodas

The Power of Repetition

- Eat at any restaurants during the week
- Eat anymore than 2500 calories a day

I also said that I would:

- Drink at least three bottles of water a day
- Eat at least one fruit a day
- Exercise each day
- Eat at least three meals a day

My penalty was that for every day that I did not follow my planner, I would have to give $25 to a charity of my choice, excluding myself, of course. This program would benefit a charity, and myself so there would be no losers. I took to Facebook and posted up my declaration because I knew a few people there who'd hold me to my words. I knew that they'd check in with me, and I knew that I could come back in thirty days and post my results.

Taking such drastic measures was necessary for me because I can be stubborn or hesitant to do something I know that needs to be done. The program worked really well, and it helped me to break some bad habits while establishing some good ones.

The Power of Repetition

Whenever you penalize yourself, the penalty should be big enough to grab your own attention. A twenty-five dollar penalty was greater than my desire to eat out or have bread. That's because a typical McDonald's meal for me only costs me about eight dollars. To think that I'd pay an additional twenty-five dollars for a cheeseburger and fries was outlandish enough to get my attention. Keep in mind that you know you better than anyone else knows you (except GOD, of course). You know what penalties would be big enough to grab your own attention, and you know who to reach out to for help reaching your desired goals. As you can see, I used this method to both break a few bad habits and establish a few good habits. I had to create a system of repetition so that I could break the cycle of unhealthy habits that I had, and I had to ignore a system that I'd followed daily in order to establish a new system of habits I wanted to have.

Here are a few tips to help you break and establish new habits in your life.
- ➔ Create a thirty-day planner, and on that

The Power of Repetition

planner, do not allow yourself to do the things you're accustomed to doing.

→ On your new planner, add new activities that you want to form as habits.

→ Penalize yourself for everyday that you fail. Make sure the penalty has a greater value to you than the habit.

→ Get a few friends involved, or get some people who are experts in that area to stand in as accountability partners for you.

→ Change your mind about the process. Don't see it as thirty days until you can go back to your old ways; see it as thirty days away from old habits while you build new habits. You have to tell yourself that the goal is to go away from the bad things. Never tell yourself that you're simply staying away for a few weeks. That's like handing an obsessed stalker a thirty-day restraining order and telling him that he can resume stalking his victims in thirty days. Whatever it is that you're trying to stay away from is something you've been stalking. Maybe it's a cheeseburger, or maybe it's some old lover's Facebook page. Whatever it is that you need to break, add it to your planner. Again, see it as something you are walking away from, not something you are fasting from; otherwise, you'll relapse as soon as those thirty days are up.

→ Educate yourself about the habits you want to break. Oftentimes, bad habits are established when we don't have the knowledge needed to keep us away from the things and people that we ought to stay away from. Learn about your mental condition and why you keep pursuing the thing or person that you've been pursuing.

→ Look for healthy alternatives. I had to stay away from white bread, so I started eating multi-grain and whole wheat breads. Of course, I didn't like the multi-grain or the whole wheat breads as much as I'd liked the white breads, so I didn't eat them with most of my meals.

→ Look for ways that your new habits will help you, and start implementing changes in your life that would require you to have those new habits. For example, let's say that you want to

The Power of Repetition

learn how to cook, but you've been putting it off for a long time. You know that if you're not inspired to cook, you probably won't cook. Try going to a homeless area each day and feeding some of the residents. This would inspire you to cook, and it would bless people who are hungry. Anytime we feel needed, that feeling will almost always be greater than our bad habits. Feeding someone else would likely be more valuable to you than your desire to lounge around the house and eat snacks.

Meditation is repetition of the mind. To meditate means to consistently run something through your mind. It means to focus on something and consider a thing (oftentimes in silence) for a specified amount of time. The purpose of meditation is to remember. That's what we do with songs. We listen to songs repeatedly, and we slowly learn the lyrics. We listen intently to what the artist is saying, and once we've learned the lyrics, we began to sing along. Anything we meditate on, we commit that thing to our hearts, and it therefore, becomes a part of us. What we've done is repetitiously listened to a song until we learned that song by heart. Whatever we meditate on, we allow that thing to dwell in us.

GOD tells us to meditate on HIS WORD. That is: GOD wants HIS WORD to dwell in us. Whatever lives in us will flow from us. For this reason, GOD also told us to guard our hearts. HE said that out of the heart flows the issues of life. So, anytime something is dancing around in our minds, we need to ask ourselves if we want that thing to get into our hearts and began to influence our thinking and our lives. If we don't want it in our lives, we should always reject the thought of it so that it does not become something that we worry about. To worry means to meditate negatively. To worry is to meditate on what Satan said as opposed to meditating on the WORD of GOD.

If you want to change what's flowing from your life, you need to change what's going into your mind. If you keep listening to secular music, surrounding yourself with worldly people, and watching shows that are sexually charged or condescending, you'll keep

The Power of Repetition

living the life that you live because you'll keep thinking the way that you think. You need to meditate on the WORD of GOD daily, and you should also make sure that you aren't meditating on things and people who are not in GOD'S will for you. I've counseled many women who were obsessed with some man because they'd meditated on the idea of having those men for a long time. Many of them started truly believing that they'd one day be with the men they were obsessing over. Because they'd spent so much time meditating about those men, they began having dreams about them. All too often, believing women will start to actually believe that their dreams are from GOD, and they'll then begin to pursue the men of their dreams. The way they had to break their obsessions was by practicing the same behaviors they'd done to establish those obsessions. They had to repeatedly and consistently tell themselves that the men they were mentally stalking were not their husbands. They had to force themselves to stop looking at those guys' social media pages; they had to stop calling the men they were obsessed with, and they had to stop entertaining the idea that they'd one day be together.

The Power of Repetition

Of course, some of the women didn't follow through. Instead, they found someone else who told them what they wanted to hear, and they began to seek counseling from those people. Years later, they were bitter because the men they'd been obsessed with had either displayed no interest in them, told them they weren't romantically interested in them, or had used them sexually.

Again, the problem was, they allowed themselves to meditate on the imaginations of their wicked hearts when they should have been casting down those imaginations and bringing them into captivity to the obedience of CHRIST JESUS. You absolutely have to be careful what you allow yourself to meditate on because that thing will get into your heart through your repetitious thinking, and it'll become one with your heart. Once it's in your heart, it'll wage war against your thinking, your reality, and your life.

The way to get a changed mind is to introduce your mind to new ways of thinking. You have to get out and meet people you ordinarily wouldn't associate with

The Power of Repetition

because of your perceptions of them. Now, don't go and put yourself in dangerous situations; instead, get out and meet people who are positive and on a path that you thought you weren't good enough to cross. The average person is intimidated by people who they feel are superior to them, and they'll purposely avoid these people out of fear of being judged by them. Don't worry about what someone else thinks of you, and don't be disheartened when you meet judgmental people who want no part of you. It's a part of the process to getting to a better you. You'll meet them again when they feel you are at eye-level with them or when they feel you have superseded their success. They'll either come and attempt to dethrone you or link up to you, but GOD will tell you how to handle them. Ask the LORD to send people in your life according to where you're going, and not where you are; people whom you can't relate to, but want to relate to.

Because I had once been judged by people who felt superior to me; all the while, being rejected by people who thought I felt superior to them (because I wasn't ashamed of my gifts), I love to talk to the women that I

The Power of Repetition

counsel about a life outside of what they know. I tell them where I've come from, where I've been, where I presently am, and where I'm going. I encourage them to get into their talents, disassociate from toxic people, and to get to know GOD better. Because they were communicating with someone they felt was doing a lot of the things they thought they weren't good enough, smart enough, or wealthy enough to do, many of them began to try on new mindsets and lifestyles. Some of these women have visited outside countries for the first time in their lives; they've started businesses, written books, and started encouraging others. They will continue to grow into the women that GOD has created them to be, and most of them will reach out to others who need encouragement to become who they were created to be. The best part of it all is GOD gets and will continue to receive the glory.

The goal is to stop looking up to people, and start looking to the hills from whence cometh your help; your help cometh from the LORD. People who feel that they are superior to you don't want to link up to

The Power of Repetition

you because you'll eventually be able to relate to them, and you'll no longer look up to them. When I'd first started out in ministry, I looked up to so many people, and I was determined to learn from them. One thing I began to see was men and women who didn't mind leading people to themselves with the sole intent of seeing their names on billboards. These characters had absolutely no interest in anyone they felt would supersede what they saw as "their success". I watched from afar as they used hungry souls and tossed them away as soon as those individuals started building or growing their own ministries. For months and years, I watched them only celebrate the people they wanted something from or the people who gave them what they wanted. Thankfully, the LORD didn't let me link up with them; instead, HE had me watching from afar. They also "publicly" thanked the people who'd praised their efforts; the very people they felt would one day contribute to their success. As soon as one of their followers started doing something they felt was greater than what they were doing, they disassociated from that person, and some of them even began spreading vicious rumors about that

The Power of Repetition

person. This is to say that you should be <u>very</u> careful who you link up to, and please don't allow yourself to look up to anyone you can reach. Be inspired, but also be watchful so you'll learn what behaviors are ungodly, and you won't participate in those behaviors. At the same time, you'll always know what level you are on and what level of life you've overcome based on the opposition that confronts you and the rank of the people who began to notice, compete with, and persecute you. Remember this: McDonald's will never compete with a small burger joint that's barely keeping its doors open. If McDonald's starts to compete with you, chances are, you are a threat to McDonald's. If McDonald's starts trying to link up to you, chances are, you are at a higher level than them. You will always know your rank based on your competition and your opposition, but it goes without saying that in ministry, you should NEVER compete with anyone. Additionally, you should never link up to anyone who's competing with you or anyone else.

You need to create new habits, and even though this isn't easy, it's definitely not as difficult as it appears to

The Power of Repetition

be. Get out and meet new people, do new things and unearth those talents that the LORD has given you. Don't be like the average person and quit the very moment someone rejects you or speaks reproachfully against you. Man's rejection is oftentimes his admission that you are as great as you believe yourself to be.

31 Days to a Renewed Mind

A renewed mind is a blessing because it gives us access to things we ordinarily didn't have access to. So, from here, you will find a 31-day journal designed to help you reach your maximum Kingdom potential. Before we get started, there are a few things you ought to know so that you can be prepared.

- The enemy will likely attempt to attack you once he realizes that you're cutting him off from another area of your life. We oftentimes break up with Satan in some areas, while we leave other parts of our hearts open to him. The goal is to close your heart to the enemy by opening it to GOD. To counterattack, simply pray and fast if you have to. Don't let him run you back into that dysfunctional relationship with him.
- Your flesh will likely oppose you after the first week. The human mind doesn't mind playing with the idea of change, but when you try to change it for real, the flesh and the limitations of your knowledge will both come together and wage war against you. The first seven days

may be a breeze, but after that, you'll likely notice yourself falling back into habits. Remember, it takes 17-21 days to break a habit. Keep going and don't give up. If you fail one day, just get back up again.
- Commit to no cursing, no gossiping, and no secular music for the next 31 days. These are things you should have put away from you anyway, but if you're still engaged in them, you need to start breaking away from them.
- Jot down your progress on each page or buy a notebook or journal and jot down your progress everyday.
- Many of these techniques may seem unorthodox or unusual, but they are effective ways to become more Kingdom minded.
- If you can't fulfill a certain assignment on the day that it's required, simply trade it out for another day that particular week.

Day 1

Pray about this, and if GOD allows you, please fast for the first day. Ask the LORD to speak to you clearly for the next 31 days. Acceptable fasts are full fasts (no food and no water) or the Daniel's fast (no meat or dairy products). Conduct this fast for 24 hours.

Spend this day talking with GOD, praying, reading your Bible, and meditating on the WORD of GOD. Let no thing and no one distract you.

Please note that you know (and believe) a certain report about your health. Please speak with your physician before entering a fast.

Day 1 Progress Report

Your Progress

_____
_____
_____
_____
_____

What Did You Learn About Yourself Today?

_____
_____
_____
_____
_____

What New Thing Will You Apply To Your Life?

_____
_____
_____
_____
_____

Day 2

Today, focus on confession. One of the obstacles that successfully hinders a lot of believers is hidden sins and secrets. Sometimes, we lie so good that we fool ourselves.

Today, take some alone time with the LORD and just tell HIM everything you feel and think. Show HIM every wound you have on your heart. If you're still mad at someone, tell GOD about it, and ask HIM to deliver you. If you have to write down names, do so, and then, lay them at the feet of GOD. Commit to never picking up those names negatively again.

Day 2 Progress Report

Your Progress

_____
_____
_____
_____
_____
_____

What Did You Learn About Yourself Today?

_____
_____
_____
_____
_____

What New Thing Will You Apply To Your Life?

_____
_____
_____
_____
_____

Day 3

Pick a room and organize it. The purpose of this exercise is to help you see the condition of your heart. The conditions we live in on the outside oftentimes reflect the conditions of our hearts.

Let everything you see speak to your heart; for example, if you notice that your place is clean to the naked eye, but you tend to be disorganized in places like your closets, cupboards, or cars, this usually indicates that you tend to deal with external issues by hiding them in your heart. You may appear okay, but behind the closed doors of your heart, there's a mess that GOD wants to clean up. Jot down what you notice so that you can take it before GOD when you pray today or tonight.

Day 3 Progress Report

Your Progress

_____
_____
_____
_____
_____
_____

What Did You Learn About Yourself Today?

_____
_____
_____
_____
_____

What New Thing Will You Apply To Your Life?

_____
_____
_____
_____
_____

Day 4

Today is positive day. No complaints today at all, and for every complaint you allow to come out of your mouth, teach yourself a lesson by giving anywhere between $5-$20 to a reputable charity.

The purpose of this exercise is to teach you just how much you complain. Most of us aren't aware of our heart's conditions until we place restrictions on ourselves.

Today, don't complain and don't listen to anyone else complain. Spend today being positive. If something or someone hurts or offends you, go to the LORD, lay their names on the altar, and remain positive.

Day 4 Progress Report

Your Progress

_____
_____
_____
_____
_____

What Did You Learn About Yourself Today?

_____
_____
_____
_____
_____

What New Thing Will You Apply To Your Life?

_____
_____
_____
_____
_____

Day 5

Today spread the love that's in you. Today, go and choose ten people and say something nice and uplifting to them. You can do this in person, over the phone, or via the Internet; it's your choice. Of course, you need to be wise with this, so don't approach complete strangers, especially if you're alone. You can do this exercise with random people that you know. Social media is a great tool because it gives you access to people you don't know without having to be in their presence.

Absolutely do not copy and paste the same text to everyone. Speak from your heart. Love is not robotic. If the person you compliment does not compliment you back or thank you, don't take offense; otherwise, you will have turned a good day until a bad day. Understand that no two people are the same.

Day 5 Progress Report

Your Progress

_____
_____
_____
_____
_____
_____

What Did You Learn About Yourself Today?

_____
_____
_____
_____
_____

What New Thing Will You Apply To Your Life?

_____
_____
_____
_____
_____

Day 6

Today is thankful day. Spend today thanking GOD for everything you see, both good and bad. Do this throughout the day. Just notice things and people, and thank GOD for whatever HE'S showing you.

Before you rest tonight, write down ten things that you've noticed today that you thank GOD for. Remember, a change in mind often requires a change in habits.

Day 6 Progress Report

Your Progress

_____
_____
_____
_____
_____
_____

What Did You Learn About Yourself Today?

_____
_____
_____
_____
_____

What New Thing Will You Apply To Your Life?

_____
_____
_____
_____
_____

Day 7

Today, wear something different than what you ordinarily would wear. Be uncomfortable today by wearing your hair different than you would, and dressing in clothes you wouldn't ordinarily dress in. Of course, please don't wear anything revealing or "sexy". Instead, wear something that's not "you". For women: No makeup today please.

The goal is to get you to think outside of the limitations you've placed on yourself. In order to do this, you will have to step outside of your comfort zone.

When you come home today, note how you felt and why you felt that way. You may notice some underlying insecurities that you have. Take them to the altar of GOD and leave them there.

Day 7 Progress Report

Your Progress

_____
_____
_____
_____
_____
_____

What Did You Learn About Yourself Today?

_____
_____
_____
_____
_____

What New Thing Will You Apply To Your Life?

_____
_____
_____
_____
_____

Day 8

Today is toss away day. Our goal today is to get you free of anything in your home that may be holding you in bondage. Go through your house and throw away anything that offends GOD. If you have music that offends HIM, toss it out. Don't give it away and don't sell it; you need to destroy it. Remember, never give what's binding you to someone else so it can bind them.

If you've worn certain undergarments while in fornication, toss them out. You are working on a new you, and everything that keeps you in yesterday needs to be tossed out today so you can be blessed tomorrow. Yes, toss out old trinkets of your slavery that were given to you by the exes (except the children, of course).
Pay attention to anything that's hard for you to throw out. If you find yourself getting offended with this advice, or me please review your relationship with whatever it is you're having trouble letting go of. Talk to the FATHER about it.

Day 8 Progress Report

Your Progress

_____
_____
_____
_____
_____
_____

What Did You Learn About Yourself Today?

_____
_____
_____
_____
_____

What New Thing Will You Apply To Your Life?

_____
_____
_____
_____
_____

Day 9

Today is donation day. If there are some things that are not keeping you in bondage, but you don't mind giving away, please take them to your nearest shelter. Today, you are blessed to be a blessing, so go and bless someone.
To be blessed, we have to learn to come outside of ourselves and help others.

The goal today is to let you feel how exhilarating it is to bless others in need. Truthfully, many people who have health issues, peace issues, or any issues could find themselves being rehabilitated if they only loaned themselves to helping others. You don't have to give much; just give whatever you can spare to a shelter. One question some of you may ask is: I know a person who needs a few things. Can't I give it to her or him?
I would say take it to the shelter instead. Sometimes, when we don't want to part with things, we give them to people that we know. Today, just bless a complete stranger.

Day 9 Progress Report

Your Progress

_____
_____
_____
_____
_____
_____

What Did You Learn About Yourself Today?

_____
_____
_____
_____
_____
_____

What New Thing Will You Apply To Your Life?

_____
_____
_____
_____
_____
_____

Day 10

Today is creative day. Do something creative today; something you enjoy doing. Now, before you declare that you are not creative, please note that every creature is creative because the CREATOR created it. We are created in the likeness of our FATHER, so you are creative. The goal is to find out where your creativeness is hiding. What did you love to do as a child? Children are very close to GOD; therefore, children usually are who they were created to be naturally. We learn to be who we evolve into as adults, but you'll notice that there were likely some things you loved doing when you were young that you don't like doing now. Today, resurrect those gifts and create something. If you're a drawer, draw something; if you're a poet, write a poem; if you're a singer, sing something, and of course, the list goes on and on.

Day 10 Progress Report

Your Progress

_____
_____
_____
_____
_____
_____

What Did You Learn About Yourself Today?

_____
_____
_____
_____
_____
_____

What New Thing Will You Apply To Your Life?

_____
_____
_____
_____
_____
_____

Day 11

Today is report card day. Normally, we have people in our lives that the enemy has placed in our lives, and these people often serve as hindrances. Today, open up a notebook and write down everyone's name that is in your life, and grade them. Ask yourself whether those people should be in your life or not. Ask yourself why you keep them around. Be uncomfortably truthful with yourself.

If there are some people in your life whose season is up, lay their names at the altar of GOD and ask HIM to sever those relationships if that be HIS will. Ask HIM to close those doors quietly, so there will be no bickering or nasty break-ups.

Don't try to remove them on your own; let GOD remove them. Be obedient to GOD and refuse to gossip or sin with those people, and they'll get up and flee in no time.

Day 11 Progress Report

Your Progress

_____
_____
_____
_____
_____
_____

What Did You Learn About Yourself Today?

_____
_____
_____
_____
_____
_____

What New Thing Will You Apply To Your Life?

_____
_____
_____
_____
_____
_____

Day 12

Today, create a list of truths about yourself; truths that you've overlooked, been too ashamed to admit, or been too busy to adhere to. Of course, these truths can be either good or bad. Make sure there are at least ten truths on this list, and make sure these are truths that you rarely visit.

The goal is to get you to not only exercise your mind, but also to dig up old talents and memories that may be beneficial to you today. Recommit to using those talents, and for old memories, look for the wisdom in those situations.

Day 12 Progress Report

Your Progress

_____
_____
_____
_____
_____
_____

What Did You Learn About Yourself Today?

_____
_____
_____
_____
_____

What New Thing Will You Apply To Your Life?

_____
_____
_____
_____
_____

Day 13

Today is a day of binding and loosing. Whatever you bind on earth is bound in Heaven, and whatever you loose on earth is loosed in Heaven. Today, consider the strongholds and generational curses that once bound your family and renounce them for your children and yourself. Make it a point to decree and declare that yesterday's strongman is no longer with you today nor will he be able to follow you, your children, and their children for the rest of their lives. Speak it over every generation of your children.

For every strongman you bind, be sure to cast it into the abyss (or pit) until the Day of Judgment. Bind all backlash, retaliation, counterattacks, and demonic reassignments in the Name of JESUS CHRIST. Call those strongmen out by name and plead the Blood of JESUS over yourself and your family.

Day 13 Progress Report

Your Progress

_____
_____
_____
_____
_____
_____

What Did You Learn About Yourself Today?

_____
_____
_____
_____
_____
_____

What New Thing Will You Apply To Your Life?

_____
_____
_____
_____
_____
_____

Day 14

Today is camera day. Find a camera in your house, and take ten photos of yourself. Now, post those photos online. Make sure it's the first ten photos that you take of yourself. Pay attention to the photos that you are uncomfortable posting. Why are you ashamed of those photos? What do you believe would happen if you were to post those photos? Who would you like to see your photos and why? Who do you not want to see your photos and why? Be honest with yourself.

The goal of today's assignment is to unearth any insecurities that may still be lingering. The average person likes photos they believe are flattering, but hates photos that show them as they really are. Look at each photo and decide what you like about that photo and what you do not like about it. Post it up whether you like it or not. The goal is to break down low self-perception and to get you to accept yourself as you are. Whatever you do, post those photos and post them publicly, not privately.

Day 14 Progress Report

Your Progress

_____
_____
_____
_____
_____
_____

What Did You Learn About Yourself Today?

_____
_____
_____
_____
_____

What New Thing Will You Apply To Your Life?

_____
_____
_____
_____
_____

Day 15

What subject are you passionate about? What are you very knowledgeable about? It's pretty easy to tell because it's likely something you will go on and on talking about if someone were to bring it up. Today, study it for thirty minutes on your computer. Conduct Google searches, read about it, and jot down your views. Be sure to finish this assignment because it's a part of tomorrow's assignment.

Make sure that whatever you are studying is in GOD'S will and can help GOD'S people.

Day 15 Progress Report

Your Progress

_____
_____
_____
_____
_____
_____

What Did You Learn About Yourself Today?

_____
_____
_____
_____
_____

What New Thing Will You Apply To Your Life?

_____
_____
_____
_____
_____

Day 16

Yesterday, you were supposed to study whatever you are passionate about and jot down some notes. Today, you're going to do something amazing. Today, you're going to start a book or an article.

Take what you've learned yesterday and what you already know, line it up with the WORD of GOD and start your book or write an article. Today, write one thousand words or more, making sure to pay attention to your words. Don't write the same thing using different words; instead, take what you know and write it in a lesson form for someone else. You decide what you want to do with whatever you've written.

If you're not a great writer, no worries. Many authors are horrible writers (I'm a publisher and editor too), but they write anyway and let their editors clean it up. Don't look at your self-imposed restrictions; just write. By the way, please note that you, not your editor, is responsible for cleaning up your book. Your editor's job is to proofread and correct whatever you've missed.

Day 16 Progress Report

Your Progress

_____
_____
_____
_____
_____

What Did You Learn About Yourself Today?

_____
_____
_____
_____
_____

What New Thing Will You Apply To Your Life?

_____
_____
_____
_____
_____

Day 17

Today is scriptural meditation day. Choose three scriptures and meditate on them today. Pray and ask the FATHER which scriptures HE wants you to read, and be sure to read them.

After you've meditated on those scriptures, ask and answer the following questions:
- What did that scripture mean?
- What new information did I learn from that scripture?
- How will I apply that teaching to my life?

Whatever you learn, take that with you for the rest of your days. Of course, you should be reading your Bible and meditating on the WORD everyday, but today, you need to read and meditate on three scriptural verses.

The goal of this assignment is to bring something into your heart that will be beneficial to your life. Believe it or not, every time you memorize a scripture and believe it as true, the wrong things in your heart and in your life begins to be evicted.

Day 17 Progress Report

Your Progress

_____
_____
_____
_____
_____

What Did You Learn About Yourself Today?

_____
_____
_____
_____
_____

What New Thing Will You Apply To Your Life?

_____
_____
_____
_____
_____

Day 18

Today's self-observation day. Review your relationships with the people closest to you, and pay attention to your behavioral patterns with each individual person. What you'll notice is that you treat each person differently, often being nicer to certain people than you are with others. Today, you need to remedy that by observing those relationships and asking yourself why you're different with each person. The most obvious thing you'll come to conclude is that everyone is different and you deal with others according to their personalities, but the truth is: whatever problematic mindsets we have, we often unleash on the people we feel are even more messed up than ourselves or the people we are jealous of.

List at least three people that you are close to, and write down how you are with each person. This will also help you to see who shouldn't be in your life because you'll notice that some people bring out the worst in you. Apologize to anyone you've spitefully misused and commit to being a better person.

Day 18 Progress Report

Your Progress

_____
_____
_____
_____
_____
_____

What Did You Learn About Yourself Today?

_____
_____
_____
_____
_____

What New Thing Will You Apply To Your Life?

_____
_____
_____
_____
_____

Day 19

Today's another charitable day. Today, go out and visit a nursing home, and be sure to ask the nurses which of the residents receive little to no visitors. Go and visit them, making sure to bring a red rose or a card to each person. Sit down and talk with them for at least fifteen minutes each. Be sure to pray and cover yourself with the blood of JESUS before entering a nursing home, as you may not know what you're walking into.

If you have to work today, and your schedule won't allow this visitation, trade this day's scheduled activity for another activity scheduled. For example, if you're off Saturday, and today is Tuesday for you, do Saturday's exercise today and do today's exercise on Saturday.

The goal is to open up your heart to help others. Once you start doing this, you won't want to stop because you'll understand the healing power of love.

Day 19 Progress Report

Your Progress

_____
_____
_____
_____
_____
_____

What Did You Learn About Yourself Today?

_____
_____
_____
_____
_____

What New Thing Will You Apply To Your Life?

_____
_____
_____
_____
_____
_____

Day 20

Today's the day to confront a fear. What are you afraid of? Be honest with yourself. Many of the beliefs and restrictions on your life right now are there because of a fear you have. That fear set up the foundation for other beliefs and fears. Today, by confronting and tearing down a fear, you will be tearing down so many walls in your mind.

If you're afraid of cats, go and handle a cat today, but be sure to do so in a controlled environment. Commit to not reacting so you won't hurt an animal because of your fear of it. Sit there with the animal until your fear is gone. You see, if you tell yourself you're simply going to confront a fear, you'll go, confront the fear, and run out of the place in fear. But if you tell yourself that you will be sitting in a place until that fear is gone, you'll open up your mind for understanding. Be sure to read some POSITIVE articles on the Internet before going to confront your fear. You simply need to change your mind; that's all.

Day 20 Progress Report

Your Progress

_____
_____
_____
_____
_____
_____

What Did You Learn About Yourself Today?

_____
_____
_____
_____
_____
_____

What New Thing Will You Apply To Your Life?

_____
_____
_____
_____
_____
_____

Day 21

Today is faith-building day. Remember, faith comes by hearing, and hearing by the WORD of GOD. Today, pick an area of your life that needs strengthening, and locate scriptures related to that area of your life. For example, if you've been diagnosed with a disease or infirmity, study some healing scriptures. Be sure to meditate on these scriptures until you know them by heart. Write the scriptures down and continue to tell yourself what GOD said as opposed to what you believe or what someone told you. Be sure to study at least three scriptures.

Today, the goal is to eradicate those strongmen that have held your mind captive. It's time to take the WORD of GOD in, believe it, and apply it.

Day 21 Progress Report

Your Progress

_____
_____
_____
_____
_____
_____

What Did You Learn About Yourself Today?

_____
_____
_____
_____
_____

What New Thing Will You Apply To Your Life?

_____
_____
_____
_____
_____

Day 22

Today is pep talk day. Today, answer the following questions:
- Do I love myself?
- Do I love GOD?
- Do I love GOD more than I love myself? If not, why?
- Do I see myself as beautiful?
- What areas of my physical body do I not see as attractive?
- What areas of my personality do I not see as attractive?
- Five things I need to be a better me are:

After you've answered all of the questions, take your answers before the altar of GOD. When the average believer discovers something about themselves that doesn't line up with GOD'S will, they attempt to hide it from themselves and GOD. They believe that by doing so, that fault will disappear, but in truth, that fault will become a default; meaning, it'll become the root of many of their decisions. Today, tell yourself and GOD the truth. Be delivered.

Day 22 Progress Report

Your Progress

_____
_____
_____
_____
_____
_____

What Did You Learn About Yourself Today?

_____
_____
_____
_____
_____
_____

What New Thing Will You Apply To Your Life?

_____
_____
_____
_____
_____
_____

Day 23

Today is character-building day. Today, go to social media and ask if anyone needs prayer. Offer to pray for them. Every time you receive a prayer request, pray for that person immediately. Be sure to share your status at least three times today to get in new prayer requests.

The goal is to get you outside of yourself once again. Character is built when we become selfless; meaning, we become more like GOD. Activities designed to flatter yourself only help you to become more selfish, or in other words, more unlike GOD. Additionally, this assignment is designed to teach you to pray for people the very minute they ask for prayer. The average believer agrees to pray for others, but forgets to do so because they put those prayers off for later. Sometimes, people need an emergency prayer, and this will help you to learn to drop what you're doing for you and do something great for someone else.

Day 23 Progress Report

Your Progress

_____
_____
_____
_____
_____
_____

What Did You Learn About Yourself Today?

_____
_____
_____
_____
_____
_____

What New Thing Will You Apply To Your Life?

_____
_____
_____
_____
_____
_____

Day 24

Today is the funeral of "I can't." Today, commit to saying "I can" all day. Find at least three things you've told yourself that you can't do and do them. Complete at least one of them, but for the other two, you should start the process today. For example, if you've told yourself that you can't swim, schedule a swimming lesson. You may not get the lesson on today, but at least it will be scheduled. If you've told yourself that you can't exercise for anymore than ten minutes, make it a point to exercise for one hour today. If you've told yourself that you can't eat a certain type of food, go and eat it. Don't just bite it; eat the entire thing. Of course, make sure it's not something you're allergic to.
Think hard and be sure to jot down three items that you've initially told yourself you couldn't do and do them.

Of course, today's exercise is geared at changing your mind by expelling the lies you've told yourself over the years.

Day 24 Progress Report

Your Progress

_____
_____
_____
_____
_____
_____

What Did You Learn About Yourself Today?

_____
_____
_____
_____
_____
_____

What New Thing Will You Apply To Your Life?

_____
_____
_____
_____
_____
_____

Day 25

Today is travel prep day. Today, make plans to go outside of the country or do something in preparation to go outside the country. I'm not telling you to go and buy a ticket; what I am saying is make future plans to travel.

The U.S. State Department's latest statistics state that more than 45 percent of Americans do not have a passport. Just like French people, Americans usually don't feel inclined to visit other countries. One of the reasons visiting another country is important is because it helps you to become more sensitive, understanding, and loving towards people from foreign lands. You won't understand foreigners until you've been a foreigner yourself.

So, today, if you don't have a passport, get one, or at least, review the information you'll need to get one. Go on a travel site and look up some plane tickets as well. Make concrete plans to travel and study the people, culture, and laws of the place you intend to travel to.

Day 25 Progress Report

Your Progress

___

What Did You Learn About Yourself Today?

___

What New Thing Will You Apply To Your Life?

___

Day 26

Today is an extension of yesterday. Traveling to another country is an awesome blessing, not just for you, but for the people you will come in contact with. Today, write down ten things you've discovered about the country you intend to travel to. Also, jot down what you plan to bring (morally and spiritually) to that country when you visit it.

Be sure to lock your travel plans in, because the average person only talks about traveling, but won't do anything to make those words manifest as reality. What I mean by locking it in is you should start saving money and asking the people you want to come with you to prepare. If you don't have a passport, and can afford to get a passport, please make plans to do so as soon as possible. You can travel via airplane or cruise ship, your choice.

Again, the goal of this assignment is to get you outside of yourself, your fears, and the "average" label.

Day 26 Progress Report

Your Progress

_____
_____
_____
_____
_____
_____

What Did You Learn About Yourself Today?

_____
_____
_____
_____
_____
_____

What New Thing Will You Apply To Your Life?

_____
_____
_____
_____
_____
_____

Day 27

Today, become a prison pen pal, but PLEASE use safety measures and wisdom. Go online and find someone to write an encouraging letter to. If you have a post office box, use that as your return address IF YOU SO CHOOSE. If you don't have a post office box, do not place your return address on the envelope as this may endanger yourself and your family. Of course, you can skip the note and go visit someone in prison, but if not, just write a long and encouraging note to someone and send it.

Again, use safety precautions and wisdom. Do not put your return address or any of your loved ones return address on the envelope. You can also go online and send emails to some prisoners, but there may be a fee involved.

GOD told us to visit the prisoners, and most of us fear doing so. This is to break that fear and help you to understand that prisoners are human beings who've made mistakes, just like yourself.

Day 27 Progress Report

Your Progress

_____
_____
_____
_____
_____
_____

What Did You Learn About Yourself Today?

_____
_____
_____
_____
_____

What New Thing Will You Apply To Your Life?

_____
_____
_____
_____
_____

Day 28

Today's a great day, and I'm sure you'll enjoy this assignment... *or not.* It depends on your relationship with money. Today, go out to eat. If you're not married, go alone. If you are married, take your spouse with you. If you have friends who are participating in this assignment, take them with you.

Find one person in that restaurant who looks like they can use a blessing and pay for their meal. Now, I know you're probably saying that this will cost you money and you don't want to separate from your money, but the love of money and the fear of losing it has crippled so many believers today. A person with a heart of giving is a person with a heart of GOD. If you and more than one person went, you can all pitch in, but don't tell the person you're paying for their food and ask the waitress or waiter not to reveal your identity. Just point someone out and tell the waiter or waitress you will be picking up their tab. Be sure to send a note to them with an encouraging message.

Day 28 Progress Report

Your Progress

_____
_____
_____
_____
_____
_____

What Did You Learn About Yourself Today?

_____
_____
_____
_____
_____

What New Thing Will You Apply To Your Life?

_____
_____
_____
_____
_____

Day 29

Today, take at least one hour and spend it with the LORD in prayer. Of course, this is one hour in addition to your normal prayer time. Use this time to confess whatever you've been feeling, renounce your fears, and ask for GOD'S help in those areas where you feel helpless.

If you have children, do this assignment when the children are at school, daycare, or asleep. Don't keep watching the clock trying to rush out of the room; instead, enjoy your time in HIS presence. Don't go to HIM with prayers you've heard others say or prayers you repetitiously pray to HIM. Pray to HIM with an open heart. Don't hold back; just take the whole you in front of GOD so that HE can make you whole again. Even if you think you're whole, go before HIM. If you do feel as if there's nothing you need to talk with HIM about, then fast today and speak with HIM. Fasting tears down the flesh and reveals what's hiding underneath.

Day 29 Progress Report

Your Progress

_____
_____
_____
_____
_____
_____

What Did You Learn About Yourself Today?

_____
_____
_____
_____
_____
_____

What New Thing Will You Apply To Your Life?

_____
_____
_____
_____
_____
_____

Day 30

Today is "let it go" day. All too often, believers have something they're planning to do or something they are holding on to that GOD wants them to let go of. Many times, it's planned court appearances, hurt feelings, retaliation plans, and so on. If you have a court case pending against someone, pray about this, but just let it go unless GOD tells you otherwise.

You'd truly be amazed at how freeing it can be to just let wrongdoers be wrong until GOD decides to repay them. If you're going through a divorce and trying to hold on to some material thing, let it go. Sometimes, releasing the wrong things is all you have to do to receive the greater blessings. If someone owes you money, forgive the debt and let them know the debt is forgiven. Now, if they were refusing to pay you the money back, use wisdom and never loan to them again unless GOD says otherwise. Today, don't repay wrong for wrong; just let go for good.

Day 30 Progress Report

Your Progress

_____
_____
_____
_____
_____
_____

What Did You Learn About Yourself Today?

_____
_____
_____
_____
_____
_____

What New Thing Will You Apply To Your Life?

_____
_____
_____
_____
_____
_____

Day 31

Congratulations! You've made it to 31 days of renewed thinking, and prayerfully, you will make the suggestions listed as a part of your daily life.

Today, create a video detailing what you've learned over the last 30 days and what you intend to take with you in life. You can keep the video private or share it at will.

Make sure you address yourself in the video. Encourage yourself in the video and keep the video so you can play it anytime you need encouraging. That's it!

I hope you've made some noticeable changes over this month long period and those changes are for the better. Continue to seek GOD in your life's journey, reading your Bible daily, going to the sanctuary as often as you can, and helping others whenever you can. Commit to creating new habits, and you'll notice a change in your thinking as the days, months, and years progress.

Day 31 Progress Report

Your Progress

_____
_____
_____
_____
_____
_____

What Did You Learn About Yourself Today?

_____
_____
_____
_____
_____

What New Thing Will You Apply To Your Life?

_____
_____
_____
_____
_____

www.ingramcontent.com/pod-product-compliance
Lightning Source LLC
Chambersburg PA
CBHW071647090426
42738CB00009B/1450